ORDER! ORDER!

Order! Order!

A biography of
The Right Honourable George Thomas
by
Ramon Hunston

MARSHALLS

Marshalls Paperbacks
Marshall Morgan & Scott
a Pentos company
1 Bath Street, London EC1V 9LB

First published 1981

British Library Cataloguing in Publication Data

Hunston, Ramon
  "Order, order".
  1. Thomas, George
  2. Statesmen – Great Britain – Biographies
  I. Title
  941.085′092′4   DA591.T/

  ISBN 0-551-00882-2

Typesetting: Nuprint Services Ltd, Harpenden, Herts.
Printed in Great Britain by Hunt Barnard Printing Ltd.,
Aylesbury, Bucks.

This book is dedicated to my wife, Jean,
without whose patience and encouragement
it would not have been written

Contents

List of Plates
between pages 68 and 69

Foreword

George Thomas is loved by all who know him inside and outside of Parliament, and his characteristic voice crying 'Order! Order!' is now recognized almost as a national institution, introducing the Programme 'Today in Parliament' on Radio 4. He is a devoted and ardent Christian, a loyal friend, and a most agreeable and amusing companion, full of high spirits, and endowed with a generous and affectionate nature. I commend this study of a great man of our times to a wide national readership.

Hailsham of St. Marylebone
House of Lords

Introduction

This book is the story of a man of our times, ordinary and unpretentious. Yet by sheer determination, he rose from a background of poverty and hardship in a Welsh mining valley to hold one of the highest positions in the land, and has served with honour and distinction as Speaker of the House of Commons.

The Right Honourable George Thomas MP achieved this success without the aid of wealth, influential friends or intrigue. He is recognised by others who have observed him at work as one of Parliament's most notable Speakers. Yet he has not lost touch with the man in the street, remains highly respected as a Member of Parliament who really cares about his constituents in Cardiff, and has two great loves in his life – Wales and Parliament. In describing his personal feelings, Mr Speaker comments, 'It is amazing what God can do with a lad from the Rhondda with a patch on his trousers!'

Three factors have moulded this man's life: his chapel background and deep Christian faith; his involvement in the National Union of Teachers; his loyalty and commitment to the Labour Party.

This book does not attempt to catalogue every event in his very full life, but tries to reveal the man himself through incidents and conversations. It seeks to introduce the reader to the warm Welsh personality of Thomas George Thomas.

I would like to acknowledge with gratitude the willingness of Mr Speaker to spend hours in conversation in the midst of a very busy Parliamentary life, giving insight into personal incidents and conversations.

I am also deeply indebted to Sir Noel Short MBE, MC, the Speaker's Secretary, and to Mr R. Canter and members of the Speaker's staff for their very valuable assistance in the production of this book.

RAMON HUNSTON

1

The Heritage

The gaunt profiles of pithead winding gear pointed like fingers to a sky far above this deep valley of South Wales known as the Rhondda. Pyramid-like slag heaps disfigured the horizon. The small towns and villages along the valley clustered together as though craving company. Row upon row of terraced houses lined narrow pavements.

Some seven miles up the Rhondda valley from Pontypridd and 20 miles from Cardiff stands Trealaw, looking across the valley to the town of Tonypandy. Here the Rhondda river flows sullenly down darkened by the coal dust as if the earth bled as men tear the coal from its depths.

This valley became home to the Thomas family. George Thomas's parents came from contrasting backgrounds, yet in the warmhearted community of the Rhondda they lived, raised their children and found brief happiness amid the grinding poverty and harsh conditions of the mining industry. George Thomas's maternal grandfather, John Tilbury was born in the pleasant Hampshire village of Clanfield. As a small child he helped gather stones to build the tiny Methodist Chapel in the village. This devotion to the Methodist church remained with John Tilbury as he went to Bristol to work. There he met Elizabeth Lloyns, fell in love and later married her. Elizabeth was an Anglican, one of their first decisions was where they should go to church since they wanted to be sure that their children grew up unconfused. Rather than worship separately Elizabeth became a Methodist.

At this time the Rhondda was not a depressed area but offered prospects of employment and prosperity. Like a magnet, it drew men and their families from many parts of the country. The coal industry was expanding, new pits were being sunk; there was the lure of jobs. It was this common factor which drew the Tilbury family from the countryside of Hampshire, and the Thomas family from their farming community in Carmarthenshire in West Wales. Whilst their backgrounds were different, both were Methodists and made sure that they joined the local chapel. The many chapels of the area were full, and provided the focus for the local community. It was in the chapel that George Thomas's father began to notice the young Tilbury girl from Hampshire. Soon they were walking out together and in due course, married. They set up home in Tonypandy, and five children were born to them. The eldest, Ada, was named after her aunt; the second, Dorothy, always known as Dolly, as a child was vivacious and full of energy, soon becoming a favourite of everyone in the street.

There was great excitement when the first son was born. He would be another breadwinner for the family; his proud father gave him a Welsh name; Emrys. The family moved to Port Talbot for two years when Dad found work there. In January 1909 the second son, George, was born; the following December a third son, Ivor. Mrs Thomas now had her hands full with five fine children. She would

sit back in the chair by the glowing fire, with George asleep
on one arm and Ivor on the other, silently thanking God
for His goodness.

Long afterwards, Mrs Thomas recounted how when
both were asleep, Ivor, the youngest would be put down in
his bed and never murmur, but George used to wake
immediately his head touched the pillow, and yell so loud
that his voice could be heard throughout the house.

After they returned to Tonypandy the happiness
gradually began to disappear, George's father began to
drink more and more heavily, until one day he left the
house and the young family. Mrs Thomas and her five
children now moved into part of a house at 139 Miskin
Road, Trealaw, a typical Rhondda street, lined with terraced houses. Some of the neatly-kept houses were three-
storeys high, housing more than one family. The Thomas
family lived in the basement. Locally known as the 'under-
houses', these were completely separate from the upper part
of the house, and partly under the main building.

George grew up in this tiny 'underhouse' which consisted of one room approximately twelve feet by ten feet with
just one window and one external door, where the family
lived and ate. There was no bathroom or indoor toilet. On
fine days Mrs Thomas did her washing outside in the
yard, bending over her scrubbing board. Leading off the
living room were two tiny windowless bedrooms. Just
outside the underhouse door stood a row of dust bins and a
small ash tip, then the ground fell away to another street
and the river. This served as George's playground. There
are still one or two people living there who remember him
playing marbles in these mean surroundings.

But the underhouse of 139 Miskin Road soon boasted a
happy family atmosphere. They were a close knit and
contented family, not because they were rich but because
they were happy in their love for each other, although

times were very hard. Each evening before the children
went to bed, Mrs Thomas would call – "Ada, Dolly,
Emrys, it's time for prayers." Gathering the two younger
boys on her knee, she would open the big family Bible, so
characteristic of any Welsh home, and read from it. Then
the children would all kneel around their mother's chair to
say their prayers.

One of George's earliest memories is of the boots of the
miners ringing on the flagstones as they made their way
home from the pit. Those lines of weary coal-blackened
men coming up the streets to their homes were a constant
reminder that coal was the only industry in the valley.
Later the men would gather in the pubs or chapels; the
coal dust washed off but on their hardened hands and
arms, or on their foreheads, the dark blue scars which are
the hallmark of the coal miner.

Aneuran Bevan once graphically described the life of
the South Wales miner: 'In other trades, there are a thousand diversions to break the monotony of work – the passing
traffic, the morning newspaper, above all, the sky, the
sunshine, the wind and the rain. The miner has none of
these. Every day for eight hours he dies, gives up a slice of
his life, literally drops out of life and buries himself. The
alarum or the 'knocker-up' calls him from his bed at
half-past four. He makes his way to the pithead. The
streets are full of shadows with white faces and black-
rimmed sunken eyes. The cold morning echoes with the
ring of hobnailed boots. The shadows have such heavy
feet.... Down below are the sudden perils – runaway
trams hurtling down the lines; frightened ponies kicking
and mauling in the dark, explosions, fire, drowning. And
if he escapes? There is a tiredness which comes as the
reward of exertion, a physical blessing which makes sleep
a matter of relaxed limbs and muscles. And there is a
tiredness which leads to stupor, which remains with you

on getting up, and which forms a dull, persistent background to your consciousness. This is the tiredness of the miner, particularly of the boy of fourteen or fifteen.who falls asleep over his meals and wakes up hours later to find that his evening has gone and there is nothing before him but bed and another day's wrestling with inert matter.'

Sunday was a special day. The Thomas family was up early; the children dressed in their best clothes and after breakfast, the door was locked and they would set off to walk to the Methodist chapel in Tonypandy. Holding the hands of George and Ivor, Mrs Thomas would lead them up the uneven stone steps of the 'gully' or passageway next to their house, up to Miskin Road and across to Tonypandy. It was the same every week; they trudged through snow in winter and perspired in summer. Nothing prevented the Thomas family from going to chapel. Chapel gave George the love of hymns that was to be a life-time pleasure. As a student he sang hymns, sometimes to the annoyance of fellow students.

Sunday was so different; no lines of weary coal-blackened men trudging home, no moan of the pit hooter early in the morning, urging still tired and sleepy men to hurry. Instead there was the singing in the chapels, from. Bethania and Caersalem; hymns in English, rousing, powerful, awe-inspiring as hundreds joined in worship; hymns in Welsh, expressing deep faith and hope. Preachers roared truth until their words echoed in the corners of darkened galleries and evoked responses from the crowded pews. 'Diolch Iddo' they cried. 'Bendigedig' someone shouted. Almost singing his words, the minister poured out the language of his faith. 'He's got the "hwyl",' they said as they left the packed chapel. Sunday was different – it was exciting, strengthening, like the bright sunshine before the cage took the miners thousands of feet down into the bowels of the earth. George's happy childhood was not even disturbed by the outbreak of the First World War. Men and women talked in solemn tones and with grim faces about death and destruction, while the oblivious five-year old played.

Many men who had kissed wife and children goodbye, were not coming home In such a closely knit community as Trealaw, families tried to comfort one another. But death was no stranger in the valleys. It was always the price men paid for coal. On occasions the pit-hooter would suddenly sound across the valley, in an incessant wail, breaking in upon the usual pattern of life. Women paled suddenly as they heard it and ran trembling to the pit. Miners on another shift would grab their tools and hurry to help. Sombre-faced men stepped blinking out of the cage into the sunlight. 'There's a bad fall.' A woman sees her neighbour still black from toil, and asks, 'Have you seen Dai?' He shakes his head and turns away. The price was not paid only in the sudden roof fall in the coal seam, or in the searing flame of an underground explosion; sometimes it was in the slow pain of breathlessness as the coal dust settled in a miner's lungs and slowly destroyed him. So many died young in those days. One could see men, old before their time, sitting pallid faced at their open doors.

As a boy, George saw many funerals. He watched wonderingly as the men stood outside the house singing the minor key Welsh hymns while the women wept inside. But his mother protected him and the other children, as best she could, from the problems they faced.

George's father served in the First World War. During the campaign in Salonika he contracted tuberculosis, dying shortly after the end of the war. Mrs Thomas sat and considered the bleak future. She concealed her feelings as best she could from the children but realised that things were going to be very difficult. There was no man to bring

in the weekly wage. She looked at the five children and
wondered how she was going to feed and clothe them now.
But she had a deep Christian faith, and believed that
somehow God would help her and provide for the needs of
the family. But she resolved not to sit at home weeping
helplessly; somehow she would provide for her family.
She dried her tears, and began to look for ways to earn
money to feed the family.

This strong determination to remain independent, to
make her own way was mysteriously communicated to her
children; in George's life it became clearly visible in later
years.

2

The Happiest Days?

Mrs Thomas sat thoughtfully in her chair. The house was quiet, the chatter of the children stilled. She stared into the glowing coals of the dying fire and suddenly decided what she must do. Before her marriage she had been a seamstress; it was a skill she never lost. Over the years she had made dresses for the girls and patched the boys' trousers, doing what every housewife in the Rhondda did to try and make ends meet. It had been specially hard during the strike of 1910 when Tonypandy had gained its reputation as a very militant centre. She remembered those days, with miners marching in the streets, great public meetings and no money coming into the home. During the strike she had kept the family looking respectable with her sewing skills. That's how she was going to earn money to provide for the children now. She would take in sewing. People soon learned that Mrs Thomas did sewing. The work began to come in. She asked neighbours and friends if they had any work for her and she made dresses, patched clothes, turned up trousers, altered curtains; anything that needed sewing.

Long after midnight and far into the still hours of early morning a solitary light gleamed at the back of Miskin Road. Mrs Thomas sewed night after night. There were times when her eyes were so tired that she could scarcely thread her needle, but she would rub her eyes and struggle on with aching fingers. Then she would lie exhausted on her bed for just a few hours before getting up again to make breakfast for the children and see them off to school.

She worked like this for years, but there were still occasions when there was not enough food to go round. The children didn't know their mother sometimes went hungry so that they could go to school with some breakfast inside them, however sparse. Although her sewing brought in money, it paid for little beyond the necessities of life; yet Mrs Thomas tried to save a few coppers so when it was one of the children's birthdays, they could have a little present. She secretly went without many things she needed so the children could be fed and clothed.

But the Thomas's were not alone in their experience of poverty. These were days of great hardship in the Rhondda, since almost everyone was poor. There was a great sense of togetherness in the valleys of South Wales. When there was trouble in the home, sickness or bereavement, neighbours helped in any way they could. In close communities such as the Rhondda, old people were not left to degenerate in the solitude of their own homes, wrapped only in the memories of the past. They were constantly visited by neighbours to see if anything was needed, and to have a friendly chat.

His first day at school was quite an ordeal for George. His mother made sure he was up early, washed and had eaten his breakfast before she took him to Trealaw Infants School. To reach the school they climbed the rather uneven steps of the 'gully' up into Miskin Road, past the chapel to the school. It was quite a forbidding prospect:

the great stone entrance arch and the lane rising to the school. Its dark stone buildings and slate roof were overshadowed by the steep mountain side behind.

George soon settled quite happily and began learning the elements of reading and writing. The classrooms were typical of the times; large high-roofed rooms leading off a central assembly hall. They could be stifling in summer and very cold in winter, but the teachers did their best. It was usual for such schools to have as many as fifty per-cent uncertificated teachers; Trealaw was no exception. George was later instrumental in gaining recognition for such unqualified teachers. Children usually left the Infants School after about two years and transferred to the adjoining junior girls' or boys' school, subsequently burnt down. George remained there until he was over ten years old.

Of course George had his problems. Once, on going to another class he was asked his name. He said very softly, 'Thomas' and then much louder, 'George Thomas sir.' 'Speak up, boy', growled the schoolmaster, and George said loud enough for all to hear, 'Thomas George Thomas, sir.' After school he ran all the way home leaping down the uneven steps of the 'gully' and rushing into the house. 'Mam, Mam', he wailed, 'why did you call me Thomas George Thomas? Everybody at school knows now, and they'll laugh at me and call me "Tommy Twice".' In the Rhondda anyone who had the same Christian name and surname was usually so nicknamed. Evan Evans was known as 'Evan Twice', for George it would be 'Tommy Twice' – which he didn't want.

'Mam' comforted her son and started to explain. 'You see George', she said, 'Mamgu, (the Welsh for grandmother) wanted you to be named after your father or your uncle Thomas.' She told him that his father's name was Zechariah from the Old Testament. 'Mam' had won the choice of names and he had been called Thomas George. George quickly cheered up – he would far rather be called 'Tommy Twice' than Zechariah!

George was a good scholar and worked hard, but his school days were not all happiness. He was small for his age and not very aggressive, and so was often the object of boyish pranks and sometimes of bullying. There dawned an awareness that life was unfair. He wondered why Dai and his sister Bronwen from up the road had new clothes and he didn't, but like so many others had to go to school with a patch on his trousers.

In the playground he listened to another boy describing a visit to the seaside to an amazed group of friends. Barry Island might be only thirty-five miles away, but for George and the others it could have been the other end of the earth. He would rush home to his mother, his lip quivering as he asked 'Mam, why can't I go?' Or when she refused him a request, 'Why can't I have it?' Mrs Thomas would sigh and wonder how such a small boy as George could understand. Ada and Dolly were older and knew how difficult things were; and Emrys would soon be old enough at thirteen to go down the pit. George and Ivor would learn the hard facts of the struggle soon enough. The memories of those hard days left an indelible mark on the young boy.

Chapel remained a great anchor for the Thomas family; every Sunday they made their way to the Methodist church. One warm day George walked down the street holding his mother's hand. He tugged at his mother as she stopped to chat with friends. Everyone they met greeted them, some of the men had a word for George; it was unthinkable to pass without a word. Then the vicar of the local Anglican church passed and Mrs Thomas greeted him. George just kept on walking. 'George' said his mother sharply. He stopped, 'George why didn't you take off your cap to the vicar?' George looked bewildered. 'But Mam he's church and we're chapel people.' His mother folded her arms. 'George, just you remember he's a man of God and you must respect all men of God. Don't ever do that again.' The subdued boy took hold of his mother's hand and they continued on their way. After this George always made sure that he raised his cap to the vicar. When 'Mam' spoke sharply she really meant it.

It was an important lesson for George, which he never forgot during later years; religious bigotry has always been repugnant to him.

The Great War finished, and the men returned from the battlefields. Many were never the same again; some were maimed, blinded or gassed – many never returned. They talked in the chapel and on street corners, and George heard strange sounding names; the Somme, and 'Wipers', as the British called the town of Ypres. They hoped for transformation in the valleys, to see the promised 'land fit for heroes'. But for George in 1919 only two things mattered: his birthday and his school examination.

Mrs Thomas called him, 'George, soon you'll be ten and I'm going to buy you a birthday present. What would you really like?' She had been saving up for this occasion, as she did for all the children's birthdays.

George thought deeply. He had always been fascinated by the big pulpit Bible in the chapel. With a flourish the minister would open the brass clasp and turn the large pages, to find the place for the Sunday reading. There was also the family Bible at home that his mother read from every night, by now showing the marks of daily use. 'Mam, I want a Bible that's my very own.' His mother rarely let her feelings show, but this request of George's was one of the most precious moments of her life.

Some of the neighbours were sarcastic when told of George's request. 'Going to be a preacher, is he, then?' But Mrs Thomas realised that her deep, personal Christian faith was being communicated in a small way to George.

The other great event for George that year was the exam for a scholarship to the Higher Grade School in Tonypandy. Perhaps if he did well, he wouldn't have to go down the pit. The usual pattern of family life in the Rhondda was for the eldest son to follow father down the pit. Obviously parents wanted the best for their children, and with the little extra money that the eldest son brought in they struggled to have their second son educated – at least one son would have a better start in life.

It was no different for the Thomas's. Emrys, George's elder brother, left school at thirteen to start work in the pit. On his first day he walked nervously to the pit with some of the men, listening to their banter. For the first time he found himself tightly packed into the cage with men and boys like himself. With a sickening drop, the cage took them deep into the earth, far from the light of day to the dark dirty sweaty world of the coal-face. When the shift finished Emrys returned to the sunlight, blackened and weary, with the taste of coal dust in his mouth. When Mrs Thomas looked at her son, Emrys seemed to have suddenly grown up beyond his thirteen years. For Emrys this became the pattern of life. From that first day down the pit he remained a miner. Great changes came in mining techniques and sophisticated safety checks were introduced but like so many others, Emrys breathed in the coal dust which settled and hardened in his lungs. Breathing became increasingly difficult, and for years he had to struggle for breath, growing weaker and weaker until at the age of 56 he developed cancer of the stomach and died. George was always aware how much he owed to Emrys, whose small wage was such a help to the family, enabling George to stay on at school.

Meanwhile the day for the scholarship examination drew nearer. At last the day came. Mrs Thomas fussed

around him. Had he got a handkerchief? She told him not
to worry. 'That's all I want you to do, George' she said,
'Just do your best.' They had said their prayers the previous night as usual, kneeling around her chair. This was
natural to them; George's mother believed fervently that
God was concerned about the ordinary things of life. His
brothers and sisters were equally anxious that he did well.
To pass the scholarship exam was the chance of a lifetime.
It was a heavy responsibility to rest on his young shoulders,
but he was determined to try to answer every question.
George sat in the classroom, nervous but hopeful, the
others all older than him. The small dark-haired boy
frowned over his examination paper, and began to write;
eventually he finished. He soon forgot its importance
playing with his friends.

But for Mrs Thomas, every day seemed an eternity as
she waited for the result. Then it came. 'George Thomas,
you have passed the scholarship', he was told at school. At
the end of lessons he ran all the way home. 'Mam, Mam,'
he shouted as he rushed into the house, 'I've passed the
scholarship.' His mother just hugged him. George's future
now lay at Tonypandy Higher Grade School. Its buildings
were similar to his present school but it was a lot further to
go, on the other side of the valley, above the main street in
Tonypandy. Today it is the Mid-Rhondda Comprehensive
School.

George was only ten and a half when he started there,
the youngest boy in the school. He was a year below
normal age for entry and always the youngest in the class
as well as the smallest. Some boys picked on him because
of his small physique; yet even as a schoolboy, he drew
friends to him. Only a week after starting at Tonypandy
School, George sensed something special in the air; even
the teachers seemed excited. There was to be a school
inspection. Of course, the inspectors had been before and

this school maintained high standards – but this was different. When the inspection day came, the pupils were warned to be faultless in their behaviour. The inspection board painstakingly assessed the educational standards of the school and recommended that the Tonypandy Higher Grade School be upgraded to Tonypandy Grammar .School. The headmaster at Tonypandy was Mr Hawkins, an Englishman. He was a reserved man, a disciplinarian with the happy knack of knowing how to get the best out of children. George Thomas will always remember the kindness of the teachers at the school. As George passed through the school, he learned much, but never lost the values that his mother had imparted to him; he learned to appreciate other people's talents.

One day George and his friends passed an old road-sweeper on their way home. His friends raised their caps to him as he brushed the leaves and bus tickets from the gutter. They explained to George why they showed him such respect. The old roadsweeper loved Welsh poetry and was himself a poet. He had entered one of his poems for the Welsh National Eisteddfod, and won the prize for best poet in Wales. To many he was merely the road-sweeper, but to George and his friends, he was a literary giant; so they raised their caps as they passed him. George and his brothers and sisters always looked forward to the occasions when Mrs Thomas took them to concerts and plays at the chapel. George usually sat enthralled. But if he was at the back of the hall, George would fidget. 'Sit still, George', his mother would whisper. 'I can't hear,' was George's reply; but he still had to sit still and stay until the end. Going back home, George would grumble, 'Why can't they speak up, I couldn't hear.' He began to realise how important it was for anyone speaking in public to throw their voice to the back of the hall. It was a lesson he remembered when he began to speak in public himself.

These concerts and drama productions were very popular in the valleys. People used to flock to them not because of any great expertise of production or finesse of acting, but because it was warm and they could meet friends. It brought a welcome change to the daily battle against hardship.

As George grew up he became more determined to try and change the society in which he lived. Whether he would seek to make these changes by becoming a chapel minister was not yet clear. What was becoming increasingly obvious to his teachers and others who knew him well was that he was developing an iron resolve, which would not be thwarted, to change things in the valley he knew so well. But George began to see a transformation in his mother. He was now sixteen; things were still hard, but better than they had been. Mrs Thomas was still taking in sewing, but Emrys was earning too, and Ada and Dolly were almost grown up. George's mother was much happier; she had been seeing more and more of a visitor, Tom Davies, who often walked back with them from chapel in Tonypandy on occasions, Mrs Thomas was beginning to laugh aloud again; it soon became obvious that Tom Davies and George's mother were attracted to each other.

Tom Davies was also a practising Christian, who had grown up in a Welsh-speaking chapel in Tonypandy. Mrs Thomas had known him since they were both children. The old friendship was now reborn, to blossom into deep affection and love. Tom Davies was known in Tonypandy as 'Tommy P.D.'. He had worked underground as a miner for a number of years but was now the winder. He controlled the cage that descended into the pit. Sometimes it was packed full of miners, and at other times with coal trucks full of glistening coal.

He was always 'Tommy P.D.'. His father before him

was a miner; and it was the usual practice for miners cutting the coal, to chalk their own mark on the trucks they sent back filled to the pit bottom. There were so many called Jones, Davies and Evans that each man had his own distinguishing mark. Tom's father used to simply put his initials on the coal tram, 'P.D.', Percy Davies. So his son was known in the colliery, the chapel and in the town as simply 'Tommy P.D.'. It was no surprise, then, when Mrs Thomas announced, 'You all know Mr Davies from Tonypandy,' and explained that he had asked her to marry him.

This could have been a traumatic moment for the Thomas children, for now they were to acquire a step-father. But Tom Davies had already won George's respect and affection, and later became a tower of strength to him. They were married in 1925 bringing new happiness to the home. They were still poor, but there was another wage coming into the home. Tom wanted his wife to stop taking in sewing and so after years of hard work, sewing far into the night, she put it aside. Of course it meant great changes. George's mother was no longer Mrs Thomas but Mrs Davies, or Mrs Tommy P.D. They moved across the valley now to live in Tonypandy.

From the very beginning Tom Davies took a close interest in George. He saw his great potential and noticed parti-cularly his absorption in history. He wanted George to stay at school until he was eighteen and get his certificate. There were times when George rebelled against this. He wanted to work, to earn money, to try and repay some of the debt he felt he owed his mother. Emrys had been working for several years, and George wanted to do the same. He wanted to make his contribution to the family. When Tom Davies talked about going to college, George said it was impossible. 'It costs a lot of money and we haven't got it.' But George wanted desperately to go on to college.

3

Days of Decision

In the 1920s the chapel was the centre of community life in the Rhondda. The chapels were full and not only on Sunday. People flocked to listen to the great preachers who thrilled their hearers with stirring sermons. One of the greatest events was the great *Cymanfa Ganu*, when people came from all the surrounding chapels, choirs visited and there would be a great hymn singing. They harmonised as they joined in; majestic tunes like *Llanfair* alternating with the minor-key harmonies of *Llef*, sounding out across the nearby streets.

But another voice was making itself heard in the Rhondda. It was heard increasingly in the chapels and on street corners; an insistent cry for social justice. The valley still knew great poverty; unemployment was high here, men stood at street corners, hands deep in their pockets. 'Indeed, I'd do anything but there's no work,'. They wanted the devastating depression lifted from the valleys; they wanted their children to have a better chance in life. This call for social justice was growing and with it came the cause of Communism. Mass unemployment and real hunger for tens of thousands of men and women – especially in South Wales – were the bitter facts of the bleak winters of the early 1930s. Out of this emerged the hunger marches, the clashes with the police, the arrests and imprisonments, and all the signs of brave but bewildered people refusing to be trodden underfoot. Most of these protest demonstrations were organised by the Communists. Trade union membership had sunk to less than four million, the lowest recorded figure between the two World Wars.

But George had more immediate concerns. A slimly-built teenager, he sat at the table at home reading over and over again *The Mill on the Floss*. He made laborious notes about it – but it was no sudden love of literature that prompted him. Each week the Young People's Society met at the chapel, and as part of the regular programme one member spoke on his or her favourite book. Now it was George's turn. When he was asked to give the short talk, for which he would have to stand up in front of his friends, he wanted to say 'no', but that was out of the question; and his mother seemed so pleased when he told her.

George sat feverishly reading the book for the last time, trying to memorise and making still more notes. It was his favourite book and he enjoyed reading it, but this was a different matter. The time to leave came quickly; he put on his coat, put his notes in his pocket, checked to make sure they were there, and set off for chapel. Although they were his friends at the meeting, a thousand fears filled his mind. Will the girls in the back row giggle? 'Will they tease me at school?' It was the first time he had ever done such a thing.

At last his moment arrived. 'George Thomas will now tell us about his favourite book.' His book shook in his hands as George rose from his seat, and made his way to the front. He reached the reading desk pulled his notes from his pocket, and smoothed them, cleared his throat nervously; and then made his first public speech – on *The Mill on the Floss*. From this small beginning, he grew in confidence each time he was asked to take part in the Young People's Society. Some in the chapel recognised the talent beginning to emerge in the boy from Trealaw.

The Methodist chapel where George and his family worshipped was to be pulled down, and a large new Central Hall was under construction in Tonypandy on the corner of the main street in Tonypandy. This new hall contrasted with surrounding chapels; it would have a main auditorium with a large gallery and a number of ancillary rooms. Meanwhile the congregation was meeting in the Judges Hall, Trealaw.

Each year a special Youth Sunday was held when a special preacher was invited. George usually enjoyed these special annual services. With scores of other young people George, now sixteen sat in the Judges' Hall, enjoying the singing items. The preacher this year was the Revd W. G. Hughes. Something was happening in the chapel that night; any whispering amongst the young people soon died away, the atmosphere became electric. The rich cadences of the preacher's Welsh accent rose and fell. He seemed like some New Testament apostle as he preached with eloquence and spiritual power. Some of the old people remembered the scenes of amazing religious fervour of the Welsh Revival of 1904, and wondered if it was all going to start again.

Mr Hughes drew to the end of his sermon, perspiration standing out on his forehead as he closed the great pulpit Bible. With profound passion he leaned forward, asking all to bow their heads in prayer, and threw out a public challenge. His eyes ranged from row to row of the young people: 'Will those young people who are prepared to commit their lives to Jesus Christ as their personal Saviour, rise from their seats and come down to the front of the hall.' He paused, waiting for a response. For a moment no one moved. Then at the back of the Judges' Hall, one young man rose, passed along the row of seats and walked resolutely to the front. It was George Thomas! Soon another young man, then another and yet other young people followed him, until there was a line of them stretching across the front of the hall.

As George listened to the preacher that night he felt as if he was talking to him alone. When he bowed his head and heard the challenge he became certain that this was a divine voice to him. 'I felt as clearly as a man could feel that God was telling me to commit myself to Him,' Although basically shy, he was convinced he had to make a public declaration of his faith.

But the hardships of the Rhondda continued. There seemed to be no shortening of the unemployed queues, no end to the poverty. It was still difficult to make ends meet in the home. Two parties were growing in power in the valley, the Labour Party and the Communist Party. As George grew in his appreciation of the problems surrounding him, an iron resolve to see changes in the valley was already developing. His mother had been deeply involved in the local Labour party for some time. George knew many of the local Labour workers for they were chapel men.

In those days in the Rhondda, the local Labour Party was led by men fired by the teachings of the Bible, often deeply involved in the chapels. Like the Old Testament prophets, they reacted with intensity against the dark social conditions around them. It was not unusual to hear a political speech prefaced by Bible quotations. Indeed a favourite starting-point for trade unionists in political meetings were Jesus' words, 'I am come that they might have life and have it more abundantly.' The language of

3

the New Testament was the language close to their hearts, and the audience understood perfectly. It was also common to sing hymns and pray publicly at political rallies. It was this climate of restive Socialism and vibrant Christianity that began to shape George's understanding of life.

Eventually the new Central Hall in Tonypandy was opened, packed to the doors with men and women whose sacrificial giving had made it possible. The Revd Rex J. Barker came to take charge of Methodism there. He was an imposing figure, but it was his sermons that captured the imagination of the large congregation. They came to listen to him, sometimes enjoying his sermons, at other times moved to tears, and on many occasions genuinely provoked. He was a fiery preacher who did not mince his words; believing that the Christian Gospel was concerned with the whole of people's lives. Whilst it is firstly a spiritual challenge to forgiveness and commitment to Christ, Mr Barker claimed that housing, education and the eradication of poverty were part of the Gospel.

From the high pulpit he would see week after week, the thin faces of the children, the patched clothes of the unemployed. Of course there were others who had prospered, and many tried to help the less fortunate. The Revd Barker would look at his congregation, remembering the homes he had visited, some little better than hovels, where families struggled to live and keep clean. He saw such pain that anger gripped him. As he preached, we would lean out of the pulpit with blazing eyes, his stentorian voice filling the Central Hall. 'Such conditions are an insult to Almighty God.' Such strong views were not always popular and later he left the ministry because of his views, though he returned to the pulpit after a few years. But he remained the minister at the Central Hall, Tonypandy, for eleven years and was followed by the Revd Cyril Gwyther who held similar views and preached in the same mould for the next twelve years.

A mutual liking and respect soon sprang up between Barker and the young George Thomas. George had a questioning mind and often asked the advice of his minister, who carefully guided him during his adolesence. The Revd Barker was a great influence on George's faith, which grew in the Youth Meetings. Sunday, George went to chapel, sometimes having to queue for an hour to get in, standing in the cold wind that funnelled down the steep-sided valley. He would turn up his coat collar and stamp his feet to keep some feeling in them. The caretaker would open the chapel doors and George would find a seat with his friends. When the minister announced the first hymn, there was a rustling of hymn books, even though most of the congregation knew the words by heart. As the organ reverberated around the chapel hundreds of voices would would begin to sing, 'Guide me, oh Thou Great Jehovah.'

4

'Lord Tonypandy'

As a teenager George desperately wanted to become a Methodist minister, for him the supreme calling. Already he was taking part in services. He longed to preach, to explain Bible truths and especially to see changes in the valley. After all the first Trade Unionists were chapel people. He had read and heard from his mother, an ardent Labour Party member, of the Tolpuddle Martyrs, and they were preachers!

George sometimes sat at home just looking into the blazing fire, 'Mam, do you know what I'd like to be?' and the words would pour out, expressing all the pent-up longings. She would put her arm round his shoulders, saying, 'George, if God wants you to be a Methodist minister, then doors will open.' But being intensely practical she added, 'we will have to look for the doors and we may have to push them open, but we will do our best.' For such a poor family, theological college was out of the question. But no doors of opportunity opened and it seemed there was no way in which George would be able to fulfil his ambition to become a Methodist minister.

There remained his strong resolve to give young people a chance in life, and to dispel the dark shadows of poverty which hung over the Rhondda. Next to preaching, teaching was the greatest work he could do. As he thought how he could influence children and transform the next generation, he decided, 'That's it; I'll be a teacher.' When George reached the sixth form, he was successful enough in the exams to qualify for college. But money was a problem, and he wanted to start earning. Together with a school friend, he applied for a post as an uncertificated teacher in Essex. George and Trevor Bennett were appointed to Fanshawe Crescent school in Dagenham, on a salary of thirty shillings (£1.50) a week, starting from the beginning of the following term.

Dagenham seemed the other side of the world. They were leaving the Rhondda, with its friendships, its closely knit community, its marvellous singing. They had no experience of teaching, and had travelled little but now they were to be in charge of a class of children, and live in lodgings.

George stood for a while in the corridor as the train pulled out of Cardiff, past Rumney Hill and across the flatter countryside around Newport. He was leaving the valley, leaving Wales, and he wasn't sure when he would be returning; but he was sure that he would eventually come back home.

Feeling very much strangers the two young men began teaching at Fanshawe Crescent School. While teaching at Dagenham George had lodgings in Chadwell Heath, which cost him £1.25 a week, leaving little for even the smallest luxury. But George remembered how much more difficult things were in the Rhondda. His brother Emrys had gone down the pit at thirteen and for years his mother had taken in sewing. Every week, George sent home half-a-crown to his mother, leaving just two and sixpence (12½p) for himself. He felt it was his duty to try to repay something for the years of hardship. In Dagenham, George used to walk for miles in the evenings, looking at the new things and sights so different from his valley. He walked because even the cost of a bus ticket had to be carefully assessed. In any case George was trying to save to get to college, and for the train fare when he wanted to go home. Week by week he struggled to put a few coppers aside.

But George was homesick as was Trevor and the other young teachers in the area. Every Tuesday evening half a dozen young Welsh exiles met together. Their only link with home was by letter; they could not phone home since working-class people in the Rhondda did not have phones. The young people from the Rhondda spent the evening talking about Llwynypia, Ferndale, Treorchy, Tonypandy, Porth – Rhondda Valley towns. They sang together. 'Trevor, play us a tune, man', and Trevor would open his battered violin case, take out his instrument and tune it. Some were Welsh folk songs cheerful and lively; others were sentimental and nostalgic. Trevor always played 'The Picture of my Mother on the Wall', a very sentimental song, which affected them all greatly. One would surreptitiously brush away a tear, another clear his throat, saying nonchalantly, 'Come on Trev, bach, play something lively.'

With what little he could save from his salary as an unqualified teacher, with help from the British Legion, and with the money his mother and stepfather scraped together, it was just possible for George to go to college. He wanted to qualify as a teacher, and gain the knowledge and skills he felt he lacked. By saving every penny he realised he could just manage it.

In 1929, George succeeded in gaining a place at University College, Southampton for a two year teacher training course. About twenty other Welsh students started at the same time. George enjoyed hearing other peoples' points of view and often went to the Debating Society meetings in college. The motions varied, 'This House is in favour of....' 'This House deplores....' Some subjects were serious, some blatantly frivolous, others political. It was an era of growing awareness of political change; many students had radical opinions and voiced then forcibly. George never took part in the debates, but sat and listened.

George simply listened intently, perhaps twisting and straightening a paper clip, a life-long habit. When the chairman called the Debating Society to order, George watched the firm, but polite, way in which it was done; he began to grasp the meanings of a proposal, amendments, seconding a motion, proposer's reply, and the many other aspects of debate. He laughed at the humour of one speaker, and the careful arguments of another. He saw how a few selected words could make a tremendous impact, and a vast torrent of irrelevancies could bore an audience.

George was very shy and as he mingled with students from every part of the county, he became intensely conscious of his very pronounced Welsh accent. There was no mistaking his origins, his sing-song accent, but there was an intensity of purpose about this young man, full of friendliness and with a charming wit. Of course he was teased about his accent and some tried to mimic his lilt but George laughed as loudly as any at the usually unsuccessful effort.

Early in his student days someone jokingly referred to him as 'Lord Tonypandy', and the name stuck throughout his university career. There are still college friends who ask, 'How is Lord Tonypandy these days?' George was always homesick. He had what Welsh students called the 'Hiraeth', the deep longing for home that the Welsh feel wherever they are. He loved the Rhondda and Wales. True there was poverty, unemployment and longer dole queues there than anywhere else in the country. But there were also the fresh, sometimes fierce breezes as you climbed the mountain until from the top of Mynydd Brithweunydd you looked down on the Rhondda, with its lines of houses snaking away towards Porth and Pontypridd.

Apart from the homesickness, which even now, impells him whenever possible to spend the weekend in his home in Cardiff, George was very happy in Southampton. In the two-year teacher training course he was taking his favourite subject was history, and the love of history has remained with him. A favourite relaxation today is to settle down in a comfortable armchair with a history book. But George was always conscious of the emptiness of his pockets and the sacrifices at home to keep him at college. Letters from home were greedily awaited – he read the news of his family avidly, and without fail there was pocket money from his mother and stepfather. It was not much, but that half-crown represented a sacrifice by his parents.

George never mentioned this allowance to anyone. He had to be sparing in the coffees he bought, but Saturday night was a problem. 'Come on George', a student would call pushing open the door of George's room, 'Get your coat, we're off down the town tonight.' But George would decline politely, 'No thanks, I want to stay in the library and read.' Sometimes they would push him to go with them. They could not understand why George would prefer to be in the library on a Saturday night. He never told them that he simply could not afford to go out.

Every Sunday during his time as a student, George made his way down to the Methodist Central Hall in Southampton. The minister, the Revd Charles Tribe, was both forthright and popular, there were queues to get into the services. Sundays were an anchor for George, his faith was undimmed and he made new friends at the Central Hall whose fellowship broadened his outlook.

George was always singing, especially the great Welsh hymns. Singing at the top of his voice in his room at the college once he heard voices shouting insistently, 'Hey, Lord Tonypandy.' Since the voices were coming from the floor above, he walked to the window and opened it. As he put his head out of the window to look up, he was surprised by a bucket of water. George quickly got the message. 'Shut up. We want to get some work done!'

The Professor of Education, Joe Cock, was a devoted Christian and a kindly man, but at times insensitive to the embarrassment he caused students by his personal challenges about religion. On one occasion, George turned to whisper to the student sitting next to him at one of Cock's lectures; something never done at that time. Professor Cock stopped speaking. 'Mr Thomas', he said 'Mr Thomas, have you any contribution to make?' Every student's eyes fastened on George as he slowly rose to his feet blushing to the roots of his hair. The professor waited, and waited. George took a deep breath and said politely, but with a strength of purpose; 'Sir, you are talking about vocational training for young people. There is only one vocation where I come from, and that's the pit!' He said it without rancour but the silence grew even more intense and Professor Cock appeared ill at ease. 'Thank you, Mr Thomas, for your contribution', the professor said after a pause, and a very embarrassed George Thomas sat down. What he had said was true. But had he made a fool of himself? At dinner with the other students that evening George tried to prevent his eyes straying to the top table where Professor Cock sat. Friends were still teasing him about his interruption to the lecture, when Professor Cock stood to make the evening's announcements: 'Mr George

Thomas is to come to my room at eight o'clock tonight. That is all, gentlemen.' He went out without a backward glance.

As soon as the professor had gone, a hubbub surrounded George. 'What have you done'? his friends asked, and others told the story of the interruption to Cock's lecture. 'Lord Tonypandy's really done it this time.'

'Come in', he heard, after knocking on the professor's door. Wondering what was going to be said to him and feverishly trying to think of any explanation, George entered. The Professor's tone of voice was friendly, and the reason for the summons even more surprising. 'Mr Thomas, I want you to come with me tomorrow to a lecture I'm giving. It will be a pleasant trip through the New Forest.' He could scarely refuse, and George left the Professor's room with a warm glow replacing the foreboding of a few moments earlier.

Next day in the car the professor turned to George and asked; 'What newspapers do you read?' George replied, '*The Daily Herald*, sir.' There was a long silence. Cock said; 'Go on', George again replied '*The Daily Herald* sir.' 'Do you mean to tell me that you don't read *The Times* or the *Telegraph* or any other newspaper?' George replied firmly 'Sir, I'm Labour and I read the *Daily Herald*.' 'You are a very foolish young man', came the unexpected reply; 'It doesn't hurt you to read other points of view. If you are to help your own cause you must broaden your reading.' At the time this seemed harsh, yet it was the beginning of a toleration for other points of view which has made George Thomas such a respected politician. He holds his own views passionately and tenaciously, but will always tolerate other views, even those diametrically opposed to his own. As Speaker of the House of Commons, he still begins the day by reading a pile of newspapers.

While at University College, George wanted to get

involved in some practical way in helping others less fortunate than himself. An opportunity presented itself. Professor Cock asked for volunteers to go to a school for the physically handicapped and George went with others to the school. But although he had seen suffering in the Rhondda, men crippled by colliery accidents, or gasping for life with the coal dust in their lungs, he was not prepared for what confronted him. He had never before seen young people like this all together; some with twisted limbs, others with misshapen heads, and some totally helpless. George, could scarcely restrain a tear. After fifteen minutes it became too much for him and he slipped quickly away and vomited. Alone, he made his way back to his room at college. He lay awake that night obsessed by the sight of these suffering young people, becoming even more determined to do something.

When he saw Profesor Cock next day he was still pale. 'Mr Thomas', said the professor, 'did you not volunteer to go to the school for the handicapped yesterday?' 'Yes, sir.' The Professor looked intently at George; 'But you disappeared.' He waited for an explanation. George, embarrassed at what had happened, yet glad to pour out his feelings, told the professor of his reaction. The stern demeanour of the professor softened. 'Mr Thomas, who is to help them if people turn away and say they can't bear it? You are called to be a teacher and this is part of your responsibility.' He walked away, leaving George feeling ashamed.

George decided he must go back to the school again. When the next opportunity came he was among the first to volunteer. He went again and again, steeling himself to overcome his feelings, yet never losing his sensitivity. He returned emotionally drained, but realising he had to subdue his own feelings. This costly experience gave him an appreciation for the nursing profession.

George was a hardworking student. Professor Cock liked him and watched him mature, recognising in him great concern for other people. He also recognised in George the potential for an academic career. With this in mind, Cock called George to his room and offered him a bursary if he would stay on at the university and take an honours degree in history.

The professor even wrote to George's parents, explaining that all fees would be paid and they would be relieved of any financial worry, if George took the degree course. They were thrilled; and George's mother wrote to tell him that of course he should take up the offer.

But George had other ideas. He was profoundly grateful for the chance but he felt that he just could not accept. The Professor pressed him hard to stay for a third year. 'Think of the doors that an honours degree would open for you.' It was a strong argument to a miner's son from the Rhondda to whom all doors had seemed tightly closed. But George was adamant that he would not stay; he wanted his teacher's certificate. 'You see, sir, I am anxious to go out and work. I feel I'm on the backs of my family. Even my brother Emrys started work in the pit when he was thirteen so that I could stay at school. I must start earning.' Professor Cock looked at the student with increased respect. 'They support me, and even send my pocket-money every week.' George stopped suddenly. In the flood of words, it had slipped out. Until now he had been very careful never to mention it.

'Your pocket money', the professor repeated. 'If you don't mind my asking, Mr Thomas, how much do you get?' George was acutely embarrassed, 'They send me two and sixpence a week sir', he said in a low voice. 'Mr Thomas, if you will stay, I'll provide your pocket money myself; and what's more your fees will all be paid. You must stay, you'll get a first in history.' But in maturing at college, George had also developed a powerful determination. He felt the time had come for him to make his contribution to the family and was not to be persuaded to stay on at college. He would get his teacher's certificate and start earning a wage, helping to educate children.

Professor Cock respected George's stand. He next said that since George was determined, if he succeeded in getting his teachers' certificate, he would get him a teaching job in London. London paid the highest wages to teachers; and Professor Cock had a friend who was a professor of history at London University. It would be possible for George, while teaching, to study for a Diploma in History, equivalent to an honours degree.

George was very grateful and became still more determined to do well in his final exams.

It was a very hot summer and the finals were held in buildings erected before the First World War. The sun beat down on the metal roof of the building making it seem like an oven. 'Ladies and gentlemen', said the invigilator, 'I realise it is extremely hot in here. However, when your results come out, the weather will be much cooler, and nobody will be concerned about the fact that you are working under heat. So you had better forget it and get on with the job. Good luck.'

George 'got on with the job' – and went for an interview in London for a teaching post. He was accepted on condition that he got an 'A' grade teacher's certificate. When the results came out, he found he had succeeded, he achieved the coveted 'A'. Now he could begin teaching.

5

Mr Thomas, sir

The year was 1931, and as he travelled to London to his
new job George was both excited and nervous. Excited
because he was going to have a class of his own, but also
wondering how East End children would react to him. He
was to teach at Rockingham Street School, near the
Elephant and Castle, just off the Old Kent Road. It was an
old building with few facilities, and the children were all
from poor homes.

But the children quickly took to their new teacher, who
had such a funny accent, and George enjoyed teaching
them. He not only saw them in class but often took them to
the London museums on Saturday mornings. This was a
voluntary exercise, but George never did it grudgingly.

One particular Saturday morning, George was taking
twenty or so boys to the Science Museum in Kensington.
He was careful to keep them together and constantly
checked the numbers. All went well until the party had to
change trains at Charing Cross underground station. To
George's dismay he found one boy was missing.

Quickly checking to discover which ten year old was

missing, and noting his name and address, George ushered the boys into a room, with the permission of a station official to whom he had explained his dilemma. Then to the amazement of the children, he had the railway official, who must have seen the humour of the situation, lock the children into the room! George Thomas was not going to lose any more children!

George decided to go to the boy's home and inform his parents, which he was not looking forward to. The boy might have gone back home. So George caught the next train back to the Elephant and Castle. As he handed in his ticket at the end of the ride, George asked if the collector had seen a small boy – 'about so high.' 'Yes', replied the collector 'he hadn't got a ticket either'; George thanked the ticket collector and hurried out. He had never before gone into the back streets off the Old Kent Road, and knew little of the home conditions of his pupils. As he turned into the narrow streets lined by terrace houses, he began to feel an intruder. Poverty was no stranger to him but what he saw appalled him.

George finally arrived at the house he was looking for and knocked on the door, wondering how to explain to the parents that he had lost their boy. But all was well; the little boy was already home, and when George explained why he had called, the parents were very grateful. They doubtless ensured that the boy did not do it again, for punishment was swift and sure. George now rushed back to the station, and caught the train back to Charing Cross where the rest of his pupils were still locked in. It was a Saturday morning that he had never forgotten.

George was living in lodgings in Coldharbour Lane, Brixton, but joined Westminster Central Hall. Although it was a long way from Brixton, George was still poor and walked all the way there! In any case he was interested in the new sights and sounds, so different from the Rhondda.

He loved going to Westminster Central Hall, and was constantly amazed at the hundreds of people who filled it to listen to the famous preacher, Dr Dinsdale Young.

As soon as he joined the Central Hall, George was given the job of handing out hymnbooks and shaking hands at the door with everyone who came to the Tuesday evening Class Meeting.

Once in three months the great Dr Young himself spoke to the class. He usually made a dramatic entrance, walking down the aisle, carrying his top hat, his rolled umbrella held out in front. He would then put his hat and umbrella on the desk before addressing the meeting.

On one such occasion Dr Young stopped to speak to the young man giving out hymn books at the door. 'Young man, what part are you from?' he asked. 'From Wales, sir', was George's reply, in the accents of his homeland. 'I can tell that, but what part of Wales?' George explained that he came from Tonypandy (some years earlier the family had moved across the river to Tonypandy). 'Mm', grunted Dr Young. 'Why did you come here?' George explained that he had been told that when he left home, he must join a chapel. 'I'd heard a lot about Central Hall, sir, and so I joined here.' 'Well bless you. Be faithful here', the Doctor said, and to George's embarrassment patted him on the head, as if he was a little boy.

One day at Rockingham Street School, George returned to his class room at lunch-time, to find a boy of ten filling his pockets with pencils and pieces of chalk. 'You're stealing', George said sternly. The boy simply stood and looked at him. He was visibly under-fed. 'Empty your pockets', George commanded, and was amazed to see how much the lad had crammed into his pockets. George had to report the incident to the Headmaster who dealt out immediate punishment. But the boy seemed to draw closer to George after this; already the young teacher had developed a reputation for fairness as well as strictness.

Whilst teaching in London, George also became more politically conscious. One night after a service in Westminster Central Hall, George came out straight into the middle of a violent demonstration. There had been strikes and marches in the Rhondda, but as a boy George had not really known what it was all about. Here he was in the middle of a surging mass of people, he had never seen anything like it.

Thousands of people were marching in protest against Ramsay McDonalds' national government. Crowds were milling around the area, slogans were yelled furiously and it looked as if things could get out of hand. To control the situation mounted police pushed into the crowds, George, an innocent in this kind of situation, found himself caught by the mass, and pushed along towards Parliament Green. Confusion grew and George, now scared, found himself close to the railings, that surrounded Parliament Green at that time. Although the railings were between four feet high, and George was no athlete, he was over those railings in a flash, and running as fast as he could to get away from the chaos. As he made his way home through the streets of south London, he realised that just as he wanted to see changes in his home valley, so the demonstrators wanted changes. But he thought, 'There's got to be a better way than violence.'

George loved London, although he desperately missed Wales. Teachers were still poorly paid, and George had no money for luxuries. He spent hours walking along the Embankment watching the pattern of life on the river Thames. He walked past those who, by their dress, certainly knew nothing of poverty, and also saw the shambling figures of alcholics and vagrants queuing for soup given by the London Embankment Mission.

One of his favourite venues was the House of Commons.

He would queue for hours if necessary on the benches lining St. Stephen's Hall, just waiting for a seat in the public gallery of the House. George became fascinated by the House as he sat waiting. His eye ranged from the high Gothic roof to the stained glass windows, still illuminated by the evening sun. He would study the statues of statesmen lining the hall and the paintings unveiled only four years previously by Stanley Baldwin. But what really interested George was the House of Commons. He always experienced an excitement as he went in to the gallery to look down at the MPs and listen to the debates. George watched famous politicians in action and the sense of drama in the House gripped him. 'It got into my blood', he comments.

George's teaching career in London was short although full of incident. After only six months a post in Cardiff became available. This put him in a dilemma. If he accepted it, he could not continue his studies, as Professor Cock wanted. On the other hand, he would be returning to Wales, and could live in Tonypandy and travel to Cardiff by train. His wages could be added to the family income, and he could repay something for the sacrifices his family had made. It was not an easy decision but he finally decided to accept the job in Cardiff – and not to continue his history studies. Just before Christmas 1931, George said goodbye to his colleagues at Rockingham Street School, looking around the classroom now decorated for Christmas for the last time. He had learned much in his first six months as a qualified teacher.

In January 1932 George travelled down the valley to Cardiff to take up his new post, at Marlborough Road School. It was a complete contrast to his previous job. The majority of his pupils now came from comfortable homes. George couldn't help comparing the situation of the Cardiff school close to the fine large houses on Penylan Hill with the narrow streets and poor homes of London's

East End.

George went into the school and reported to the Headmaster, Mr Francis. 'Mr Thomas', the headmaster said, 'you'll be taking the first class.' George realised that this was the lowest age group in the school. 'But Mr Francis I am trained to teach seniors.' 'Yes, that is very interesting but here you are taking the seven-year olds.' The headmaster handed him the timetable for his class and as he studied it, one subject dismayed him. 'Mr Francis, it says here I have to teach music, and I can't do that.' Mr Francis studied the new teacher for a moment, and then said firmly; 'Can't you? Well you had better shut the door of your classroom and do your best.' George did his best. His music lessons consisted of teaching the children to sing Welsh folk songs and the old hymns that he loved so much – always making sure the door was firmly closed!

But worse was to come. He found he had to teach these young children to read. He looked up from his timetable, 'Sir, I've never been taught how to teach young children to read. I don't know how to do it.' George felt very inadequate. Mr Francis put him at his ease, and explained that the school used the 'look and say' method. 'I'll tell you what we'll do, Mr Thomas', he said. 'I'll take your class for reading for the first three lessons and you can watch what I do.'

He soon settled happily into the school. As the youngest member of the staff by twenty years, he was expected to take voluntary sports duties on Saturday mornings. It was considered a privilege to undertake the work. 'It was a great privilege to have total strangers place their children in your care and allow you to influence their thinking, their character and their life.'

One of George's pupils at Marlborough Road School was the well-known doctor-poet Dannie Abse. He remembers his one-time school teacher as 'kindly, avuncular, rather strict about a good appearance.'

One morning after the Scripture lesson, George was teaching arithmetic. He noticed that one little boy was paying scant attention. He was pale and suddenly fell from his desk into a little heap on the floor. George rushed to him and gently picked him up. He had fainted. After bringing him round, George asked kindly, 'What did you have for breakfast this morning?' The boy tearfully shook his head, and George realised that he had had no breakfast. Later that morning when the children had their milk, George noticed that this same boy didn't have any. George realised then the boy's family couldn't afford it. Children paid a half-penny a day for milk – too much for this family. But now George secretly ensured that the boy always had his bottle of milk like everyone else.

Although Marlborough Street School was in a comfortably off area and most of the children were well-provided for, some were desperately needy. George could identify with them from his own childhood poverty. Returning to live in Tonypandy, things had changed little in the intervening period. There was still the poverty and hardship all around. George now followed his mother's footsteps and joined the local Labour Party. They were both active in the local Party organisation, constantly attempting to further their ideals. They worked hard and George soon gained a reputation as an ardent Party worker. Although he regularly attended the Party meetings changes were slow in coming.

Another political party was calling vociferously for social justice; the Communist Party. George was still deeply involved in the chapel, and examined the concern of Christianity for other people; but he was hearing talk of man's equality in all things. The ideals of the Communist Party first attracted, then fascinated him. He was attracted not so much by Marxist ideology and thinking, as by the organisational militancy. Exponents of Communism in the Rhondda seemed prepared to achieve changes in social conditions in the valley, whatever the cost. They wanted changes now, not later. This immediacy captured George's imagination – he too wanted change, and wanted it now. But there were aspects of militant Marxism he could not reconcile with his very real Christian faith. George became dissatisfied and bewildered.

George went to see the pastor, the Revd Rex Barker. They were both concerned about the conditions around them, and both had a fervent Christian faith. George poured out his feelings to his minister. 'Why is it taking so long to get things done? Look at the Communist Party. Perhaps that is what we need to change things round here.' Gently but firmly, Barker talked to George, guiding his thinking. George began to realise that the militancy of the Communist Party was not the way. The extremism of Communism and the materialism of Marxism were hostile to everything that he believed in the New Testament, and contrary to his Christian faith.

Although sorely tempted to join the Communist Party, that night's conversation clarified his thinking. Never again was he attracted in that direction. Before George left the minister's house, they knelt and prayed most fervently for God's blessing and guidance.

They shook hands and George went out into the night. It was late, and few people were about. George walked home deep in thought. Strolling slowly past the terraced houses he knew so well, he made a determined resolve. Nothing would change his faith; and he would do his utmost to see changes in the valley. He would be a Christian Socialist. Hands thrust deep into his pockets, he walked on. The depression that had hung over him was gone; the doubts and questionings were resolved. He would not only be a Labour Party member, but would become a Party Worker. He determined to be more and more active in promoting his ideals.

Today, George Thomas still sees Christianity as the only effective answer to Communism. In his book *The Christian Heritage* he says; 'Christianity has as great a vested interest in social justice for the masses as Communism has, but, of course, it looks for more. It is a fundamental fallacy of modern Communism that it believes that economic well-being is the end all and be all of life. This philosophy is all very well for the starving underprivileged masses of the world. It gains their initial loyalty. But it is hopelessly inadequate as an ultimate basis for life, as they are beginning to find.

'Because man does not "live by bread alone", the theories of Karl Marx are insufficient to meet our needs.'

'Christians in society will be revolutionaries as long as the world rejects Christ's teaching. His activities are bound to favour the coming of a kingdom where status does not depend on wealth, where privilege exists only as an opportunity to serve, and where fullness of life is freely available to all. This is the Christian heritage intended for men of every generation.

'Our first concern is bound to be for those who are not able to fight to ensure their own advance. To exalt those "of low degree" and to fill the hungry "with good things" cannot be done by singing hymns or even by prayer alone. This is something that requires dedicated men in politics. A blind man can see that it means Christians must be prepared to put the elementary needs of the human family before privilege for the few. There is something offensive in our parade of luxury in a world where two out of every three people suffer from malnutrition. The Christian answer to advancing Communism is for us to identify ourselves utterly and absolutely with the hungry and neglected folk for whom Christ proclaimed the "acceptable year of the Lord".

'The truth is that we can only "out-love" the Communists
in concern for the underprivileged; we cannot hope either
to outwit or to defeat them by our military might. This calls
for service in politics disciplined by the constraint of Christ,
and this is only possible when politicians are practising
and worshipping members of a Church fellowship.

'It is quite impossible for anyone to survive the cynicism
and the false values and to follow an unswerving path of
service to the humble, poor and needy unless he draws his
strength from the fellowship of Christian believers. The
vision of the Kingdom will fade and disappear if his
highest loyalty is to Party politics. The man whose vision
is bounded by Party advantage alone is the one least likely
to serve either the community or his Party with best effect.
Communism seeks to provide substitutes for public worship and Church fellowship. Our obligation is to prove by
hard work, by bold social planning and by selfless giving
that the dynamic of Christ has no equal anywhere or at any
time. This is the only safe basis on which we dare to build a
social order of "human equality", and the sharing on an
equal basis of the rights and privileges of life for all".'

George Thomas remained as a valued and respected
member of staff at Marlborough Street School. At the
outbreak of World War Two several of the male teachers
were called up, but George remained. Since he was classed
'grade 3' he was rejected on medical grounds.

The 'phoney war' of 1939 passed into blitz. Dunkirk
passed into history and the war came nearer to the British
population. Bombs fell on Cardiff as on so many other
British cities. The Cardiff docks were a prime target but
there was indiscriminate bombing too, and one night
Marlborough Road School was hit. George was sent to the
nearby Roath Park School. Roath Park itself is a long,
narrow recreation area with a wood, a lake where boys

enjoy fishing, and formal gardens, and football pitches. The school is a red-brick building surrounded by a playground. Here George made another beginning, now as an experienced and respected teacher.

Roath Park School was not so well equipped as Marlborough Road and one of the things that really irritated George was the gas lighting in the classrooms. It was totally inadequate, the lights giving only a circle of light immediately beneath, then leaving the rest of the room in shadow. On dull November afternoons George's class became a study in light and shadow!

At Roath Park, George indicated that he enjoyed taking the Scripture lessons, so it was soon arranged that he should teach Scripture to the whole school. With a smile he reminisces, 'My colleagues were only too happy to leave things to me.'

6

'You should be
a preacher, George'

George was glad to be home in Tonypandy. All the time he
had been away he had been homesick. Now living back in
Tonypandy, he was in his regular place in the Central Hall
in Tonypandy every Sunday. He was glad to be back with
his old friends.

During George's youth the Methodist local preachers in
the valleys varied in character. Some had received an
extensive formal education and could give a learned dis-
course. Others had left school at an early age to go down
the pit. They were self-taught, and if they lacked polish
they made up for it by their sincere faith.

One such local preacher was Owen Buckley, an old
miner who had seen great hardship in his youth. His
formal education ended at the age of ten when he first went
down the pit to hew coal. But Owen had taught himself in
later life, using the Bible as a text book. He was a friend of
George Thomas' uncle George, after whom George
Thomas was named. George was fascinated to know that
Owen could recite, word-perfect, the whole Book of

Psalms. More than that, he could pick any particular psalm or several of the psalms not in consecutive order and repeat them. George shook his head in amazement as Owen quoted by heart so much of the Bible as he preached.

Owen used to say, 'You know, George, the Bible has been my university.' It had given the old miner a mastery of spoken English and pulpit oratory, which, allied to his natural flair for public speaking and his Celtic fervour had made him a respected local preacher in the small towns of the Rhondda Valley and in adjoining areas. His hands were gnarled by years of toil underground, and had the blue scars that were the badges of his trade. But when he stood in the pulpit of a Methodist chapel and opened the great Bible, his dignity and reverence became obvious.

Owen influenced many people during his years as a preacher and his impact upon George was far-reaching. Not long after George returned to live in Tonypandy Owen mentioned to him that he was going to preach in the little Methodist chapel in nearby Llwynypia the next Sunday. 'George, I'd like you to come with me and read the lesson in the service.' George readily agreed as he always enjoyed listening to Owen preach.

Owen began the service, and at the appropriate moment he introduced George and asked him to step into the pulpit and read the lesson. George climbed up, opened the Bible, and began to read. He felt a strange stirring of his emotions as he stood in the pulpit and read the Bible. As he took his seat again the words of his mother flooded into his mind; 'George, if God wants you to be a Methodist minister, doors will open.'

After the service, the old miner and the young teacher left together. As they went on their way home, Owen turned to George, 'Next Sunday I'm going up to Treherbert', (another small town in the Rhondda). 'I'll be preaching there, and I'd like you to read the lesson again.

But this time I want you to say the opening prayer as well.'
George readily agreed, but later had misgivings. He had
not led a congregation in prayer before, and was afraid that
praying extempore, he would not know what to say. As
Sunday drew nearer, George's unease grew.

Owen and George arrived at the Methodist chapel in
Treherbert, and the service began. When it was time
George stood, closed his eyes and endeavoured to forget
everyone else, and simply speak to God. The faith and
sincerity of this young teacher brought a response from
the congregation, Owen Buckley preached that night as
well as ever. At the close of the service, many members of
the congregation warmly thanked Owen and his young
protege. When Owen and George set off home to
Tonypandy, Owen seemed preoccupied, and not his usual
ebullient self. They walked on in silence until Owen
suddenly stopped and turned to his companion. 'George, I
think you should ask yourself whether God wants you to
be a preacher.' Owen continued, 'Listening to you tonight,
George, I think that you should be a preacher.' After
thinking over what Owen had said for some time, George
went to see his minister. He explained to Mr Barker his
longings over many years to be a Methodist minister.
'Mr Barker', said George finally, 'Somehow I think God is
calling me to be a preacher.' Mr Barker was thrilled, and
did all he could to encourage the young teacher to develop
his preaching.

George wanted to be recognised as a Methodist local
preacher, and for this he was required to read all John
Wesley's sermons and preach a trial sermon. The date was
fixed for George's trial sermon, and as it drew near he
became quite nervous. 'It's like taking your exam in
college', he said.

It was on a Tuesday evening so that the other local
preachers could be present. Most Sundays they were

scattered throughout the valley, and during the day they would be hundreds of feet underground, black with coal-dust streaked by rivulets of sweat. But now bathed, and wearing a change of clothes they had come to listen to George Thomas. 'Who's the preacher tonight, then?' It's young George Thomas from Tonypandy, you know – Tommy P.D.'s stepson – he teaches down in Cardiff.'

Most of the people there knew George. Owen Buckley would be there listening, and of course the Superintendent minister. As George began he sensed the encouragement of the people. 'Amen', they murmured as he made his state-ments of belief. As he continued, the nervousness slipped away; he was doing what he had dreamed of – standing before a congregation and preaching.

George concluded his sermon and sat down. It was now time for other local preachers to throw questions at the aspiring preacher. George was questioned about his faith, his personal experience and about John Wesley's sermons. With joy and relief George realised that he had passed the trial and was now an accredited Methodist local preacher. 'Goodnight, George, you did well', they said and with a special satisfaction he walked out into the night.

George's life now took on an established pattern. Each week-day he travelled by train to Cardiff to teach; often on Saturday morning he was back down in Cardiff for some school activity; on Sunday he was preaching at some chapel. He began to miss his friends at Tonypandy Central Hall, as he was rarely there on Sundays because of his new commitments, but decided he must not lose touch with his home chapel and the minister he respected so much.

Treherbert Methodist Chapel holds many memories for George Thomas. One Sunday stands out. Although he was a schoolmaster in Cardiff, wages were still low, and George didn't have much money left when he had paid his expenses and his contribution to the home. George felt in his pocket and counted out his financial resourses. It was easy, he had just three pennies! He looked at the three coins in the palm of his hand and wondered what to do. The bus fare was three pence in each direction. George's dilemma was whether to walk there and ride back or vice versa. He decided to travel to the service by bus, so as to be punctual but to walk back – a distance of eight miles. After conducting the service at Treherbert he said goodnight and set off home. At first it was invigorating to walk, but Tonypandy seemed to get further and further away. 'I wasn't the first Methodist preacher to walk miles after preaching.'

Although his preaching seemed to contrast with his teaching and his political career, it brought together all his vital interests. His regular Sunday preaching gave him a platform presence and strengthened him as a public speaker. His congregation varied in size; sometimes in a small village he would preach to a handful of people, and on other occasions he would stand in a pulpit in front of hundreds. He became used to facing crowds of people.

There were many local preachers in the Rhondda and on any Sunday morning you could see them standing at bus stops or waiting for the train to take them down the valley.

George was becoming quite well known, and when visitors from towns in adjoining valleys heard him preach, they invited him to take services in their own chapels. He was often seen standing with the others at Tonypandy station on a Sunday morning, or for the conveniently-timed train on a Sunday evening, that all the preachers usually travelled on.

One Sunday, George had been preaching in the Merthyr Valley and returned with many others on the 'Preachers Express.' It was in fact a slow train, which stopped at every little station in the winding valley, and was pulled by

a small, wheezing steam engine. The ticket collector
smiled as he saw the preachers coming home, dressed in
their Sunday best, several carrying large Bibles. George
gave him his ticket and the ticket-collector grinned. 'Do
you know what I call this train, George?' He looked
puzzled. 'I call it the "return of the Empties",' and he
laughed out loud. All the preachers were coming back
having given out their sermons.

The sense of a calling to preach was something precious
to George. It was not just a hobby or a pleasure; his
preaching was and remains an integral part of his life.
George Thomas has continued preaching Sunday by
Sunday. Recently he was preaching in a chapel in the Vale
of Glamorgan. There was a large congregation and a note
was passed up to the guest preacher in the pulpit. George
unfolded it and his face lit up with pleasure as he read it.
His eyes searched the congregation. The note said simply.
'Dear Mr Thomas, your old history teacher, Miss Cox, is
in the congregation.' When he stood to preach, George
read out the note to the congregation and paid tribute to
the old lady sitting in the pew.

'Do you know, I get a lot of invitations to preach because
I am the Speaker of the House of Commons. People come
to see if I've got two heads or one! Then they find that I'm
just like anyone else', and he adds with dignity, 'and it's
just the same old Gospel message I preach.'

Later in local Party organisations and in the House of
Commons, George met many who had begun in the
chapels, but when the demands of public and political life
told upon them, they relinquished their links with the
chapels, while still trying to keep their faith alive. Such
meetings only strengthened George's resolve – he would
keep preaching every Sunday he could. In fact Sunday
would be strange if he was not in chapel.

George has preached in other parts of the world,

including almost every state in America. In Easter 1979 he was the honoured guest preacher at a great Methodist Convention in Massachusetts.

7

First steps into the lime-light

Having grown up in the Rhondda valley with its poverty and hardship, the degradation of unemployment was the background of George's youth. As a teenager, he watched the great marches through the streets of the Rhondda by men trying to do something to alter their situation. With his Methodist background and his mother's activity in the local Labour Party, it was natural for the Trade Union Movement to play a part in George Thomas's life.

George had been both thrilled and horrified during the history lessons at Tonypandy Grammar School, as he heard about the origin of the trade unions. He sat enthralled as Miss Cox taught the class about the Methodist Tolpuddle Martyrs deported to Australia in 1839 for daring to form an agricultural workers' union, based on the principles they found in the New Testament. Because coal mining was the only industry in George's youthful years, one union, the South Wales Miners Federation dominated. Its leaders were all men from the chapels. Some had left the chapels and a decline in attendance on Sunday became more and more obvious. But they maintained a respect for what the chapels stood for.

It was not uncommon in the great miners' meetings held during the dark years of the depression in the 1920's and 1930's for the leaders to quote long passages from the Bible in support of their demands for social justice. Of course, their audience was familiar with the New Testament, and loved to sing the old hymns. It was these miners' rallies and meetings with these religious overtones which so deeply influenced George, that in his own political meetings he always included hymns.

As an uncertificated teacher at Dagenham George was not able to join a union. But in his first week as a qualified teacher, George joined the National Union of Teachers. He was proud that at last he was a member of a trade union. There was never any question in his mind about joining; for it had been ingrained into him from an early age, that it was the natural thing to do. He had been a member of the National Union of Teachers for only six months when he returned to Cardiff to teach at Marlborough Road School. Although somewhat shy he was not content to be a mere passenger in the trade union. He wanted to do something positive to make the ideals that had burned so strongly in him come true.

He made a point of attending union meetings regularly, and it was soon obvious that he was keen to work for the union, so he was given his first job, as collector for union dues at Marlborough Street School. The highest pay for a class teacher was £366 a year; as a newly-qualified member of staff, George's salary was just £200 a year. Conscientiously, George collected the union dues, £1 per year from his colleagues.

George seemed to have an unquenchable thirst for trying to change the darkness and depression of his home town and the Rhondda Valley.

Inspired by his mother's example, George also became a

local Labour Party member. There are still those today
who remember Mrs Thomas coming to their front door
with a basket of used shoes that she had been given to
distribute. One elderly lady still living in Miskin Road,
Trealaw comments, 'Poor – we were so poor that we had
many more dinner times than dinners!'

At Labour Party meetings a new voice was being heard
more and more frequently, and what he said was noticed.
The young teacher from Cardiff was increasingly in
demand for his political speeches. Men considerably older
than George began to recognise in him a potential leader
in local politics. His speeches were fiery without being
offensive, and showed an uncompromising strength when
he felt he was right. His rise to local prominence was
meteoric and he soon became the chairman of the Labour
Party for Mid-Rhondda, a considerable achievement for
such a young and comparatively inexperienced man.

George's political involvement was also developed in
the National Union of Teachers. At the first union meeting
he attended in Cardiff, his voice was heard and made an
immediate impact. As he rose nervously to his feet people
turned to look at the newcomer. The young teacher did
not rise on a point of order or to make some trivial point of
argument, but plunged immediately into controversy. The
meeting hushed as George Thomas had the temerity to
table a resolution for the National Conference. It dealt
with the needs of the unemployed; and as he spoke, surprise gave way to admiration as his listeners realised that
here was a young teacher with a very deep concern. That
night George Thomas spoke forcefully but without brash-
ness, incisively but without rudeness and his colleagues
began to take notice.

'George', one said next day, 'that was a great speech at
the union meeting, I didn't think you could put it over like
that.'

This was not a solitary opinion, for his ability as a speaker was soon recognised by the Cardiff Association of Teachers. He was noticed as a speaker who could present an argument clearly and effectively, and was devastating in debate. The years in Southampton when, as a student, he had attended the Debating Society meetings to observe and learn, were beginning to bear fruit. His grasp of procedure, which he had seen in operation as he sat in the Visitor's Gallery of the House of Commons, was increasingly useful. The Cardiff Association of Teachers asked George to become the Public Relations officer. He served in this capacity for five years, bringing him more into the public eye. Small paragraphs appeared in the *Western Mail* or in the evening paper *South Wales Echo*, quoting the Public Relations Officer of the Cardiff Association of Teachers.

He became increasingly confident in dealing with the public and presenting the teachers' point of view. Looking back, he says, 'This was a tremendous preparation for my political career.'

Five years later George was asked to stand for election as the President of the Cardiff Teachers Association. To be considered for the office was quite an achievment for George, but when the count was taken, to his surprise and pleasure, he was elected.

George was not only a major influence in the local union but was becoming very popular. He had the knack of being able to put people at their ease and won many friends by his natural charm. Even those who opposed his views admired his straitforwardness in dealing with a situation. It was at this time that some of his colleagues began referring to him as 'our George', an affectionate term that has persisted. Later, as a Member of Parliment, his constituents called him this, even during the General Election of 1978. In his wig and ceremonial dress Mr

Speaker may dominate the scene at the House of Commons; but in Cardiff West, his constituency, he is still 'our George.'

It was during the dark years of the Second World War that George served as President of the Cardiff Teachers Association. It was not the happiest time for him. He saw colleagues and friends leave the school for active service. Some called in to the school for an hour to see him when in Cardiff on leave. Many of them looked terribly young in their khaki battledress, RAF blue, or Naval uniform. George failed the medical exam and was classed as grade three, so he remained behind in Cardiff. He continued teaching, and was also appointed a special policeman.

At the union branch meetings it was customary to read out the names of teachers who had died in the fighting or in bombing raids. As President it was George's duty to undertake the task, and to ask the meeting to stand in honour of their colleagues. At almost every meeting George had to read out names. Often a lump would come into his throat, as he came to the name of a man well-known to him. He could not help thinking of the children deprived of a father, of the mother struggling to care for the family. George would always remember the poverty of his own childhood.

For some years, even before he became President of the Cardiff Teachers Association, George had hurled himself unreservedly into the Class Teachers Movement, a strong group within the union, especially concerned with actually teaching in the classrooms. George strove to press the needs and point of view of the class teachers and the concerns of the rank-and-file of teachers.

He was effective, too, and speaking appointments soon took him beyond Cardiff into other areas of Wales. Because of his union involvement and his increasing reputation in the valleys as a Labour Party member, particularly in the Mid Rhondda area, in 1942 George was asked to stand for election to the Executive of National Union of Teachers. The request startled and challenged him. At the age of 34 he was being asked to stand for election to his union Executive. His friends urged him on. 'You can do it, George.'

George agreed to stand as one of the four representatives from the whole of Wales; and when the result was announced George Thomas was one of the four elected. In 1943 he duly joined the thirty strong Executive of the NUT. His ideals to see children have a better chance in life, now reached out beyond the narrow limits of the Rhondda valley, or even the confines of the city of Cardiff – he now began to speak to the whole country.

His ready wit and infectious humour coupled with his incisive understanding of matters and made him a formidable opponent in debate, but also a true friend. George was in great demand as a speaker, and as a member of the Executive he travelled throughout the country addressing teachers' meetings.

George quickly became aware of how careful he must be in public speeches and off-the-cuff comments. The press were beginning to report what the young member of the Executive was saying. George's Celtic fervour would sometimes grip him, and in speaking to an audience about things he felt strongly it was easy to let his words just run on. What was said in the heat of the moment could look very different in cold print next morning! 'I began to realise how careful I must be not to exaggerate – after all, every Welshman exaggerates!'

As George travelled around the country speaking he found it a pleasure to make new friends. He was visiting Newcastle-upon-Tyne on one occasion, and having addressed the meeting, was preparing to leave for home. 'Mr Thomas', someone said, 'I'd like to give you a present to take back', and gave a package very carefully to George. It was one fresh egg!

George thanked the giver politely and left, carrying the egg delicately. 'It seems laughable now', he says, 'but remember it was wartime, and we were all on rations – my egg was an extra treasure!' This occurred when 2oz of butter, 4oz of margarine and one egg were one person's ration for a week!

One of the great stands he made at this time concerned school meals. George always wanted the best for children, and endorsed totally that children should have school meals. He never forgot seeing the little boy who had come to school without anything to eat lying crumpled on the floor of the classroom. But he did not recognize it as the teachers' responsibility to superintend school meals, and said so forcibly wherever he went to speak for the union.

This question, which is still debated, was not because George had no interest in children other than educating them, or because he didn't want the extra duties. It was because he believed the teaching profession to be one of the noblest callings. He remembered his own struggles to become a teacher in Dagenham; the struggle to pay his way through college, and the pride of achievement when he did qualify. 'As I look back, I think that I was misguided in the emphasis that I put, that it was not the teachers' responsibility to look after the meals,' he reminisces.

In talking of those days he says, 'We had great battles over salaries then, but that's nothing new. But the thought of striking never came to our minds.' George constantly stressed that they had an obligation to put the children first, themselves second. 'I can think of a hundred times when it was said at the Conference of the National Union of Teachers, that "we are here to serve the children of this generation." We went on to say that therefore we are entitled to fair living standards. The thought of prejudicing a child's chances at examinations by deliberately choosing the most awkward moment to withdraw one's labour was as remote from us as the moon is from earth.'

Another major campaign that George fought which helped transform the standards of the teaching profession was for the recognition of uncertificated teachers. When George was at Junior School, it was quite common, certainly in Wales, for as many as half the staff to be uncertificated. He remembered vividly starting his own teaching career as an untried eighteen year-old straight from school. It couldn't be right. On the other hand, there were uncertificated teachers, especially in remote rural areas, who had served faithfully and effectively for many years. Such a teacher could devote a lifetime to teaching yet never receive official recognition. Some seemed to be born teachers and could communicate with children even better than some with formal qualifications. Of course, there were also those who could not really educate children, and it would be better if they left the profession. The problem that George and the Executive faced was how to correct the situation without losing teachers of quality. They wanted to upgrade their profession, and to give recognition where it was deserved.

The plan that George worked out seemed to promise a long-term solution, and after full discussion it was agreed. After twenty years of experience, an uncertificated teacher would be recognised as qualified, but no more uncertificated teachers would be engaged. The campaign succeeded, today there are no unqualified teachers as there were in George's youth.

Although he had taken only a two-year course at Southampton to qualify as a teacher, George believed the training of teachers ought to be a three year course. The National Executive agreed with him that teaching was as much a profession as law or medicine, and therefore should be considered alongside the other graduate professions. Because George was convinced that high standards were vital for his profession, he campaigned energetically to see a three year course and succeeded.

The miner's son from the Rhondda was making a considerable impact on the teaching profession. He was rising in the estimation of his colleagues, yet managed to retain a simple sincerity all the more startling when it was realised that it had happened in the space of less than three years.

When he had been a member of the Executive for only two years, he received requests from all over the country to allow his name to be put forward as a candidate for the Union Presidency. It appears that there was a strong body of opinion prepared to back him. He was very reluctant. His teaching experience was not as extensive as most on the Executive and he still felt he was very much 'the new boy.' But 'the new boy' had made an impact. His oratory in meetings could be fiery and emotional, and people sometimes stood to cheer as his Celtic ardour gripped their imagination. Yet in discussion he could quickly grip the vital issues of a problem.

'Why don't you allow yourself to be nominated, George', his friends said. 'You've got a lot of support.' At last he agreed, and his name went on to the ballot-paper, although it seemed to him a great impertinence. 'Only a young man would have the cheek to do it', he comments. When nominations closed, there were five candidates and George really felt that he had gone too far this time. This was not false modesty and lack of courage, for George Thomas had an iron resolve that had been forged in the flames of hardship and fashioned on the anvil of poverty. But friends told him he had done the right thing and that he had a good chance of success.

One of his greatest supporters was his mother. The years were leaving their mark on her but she was as active as ever in local politics. She had seen her son begin his political life in the local Labour Party, heard his speeches, and travelled to support him when she could; now George was reaching out for the pinnacle of success in his union.

There was disappointment; he had not succeeded but what was remarkable was how well he had done in his first election for the Presidency. The new President was Ralph Morley, who came from Southampton and had been a Member of Parliament. He was greatly respected and accustomed to public life; he would fulfil his duties as President admirably. The runner-up was George Thomas from Tonypandy. George was amazed at the result, especially as it meant his certain success next year. The usual practice was that the runner-up became President the following year.

As he travelled on the train up the familar route from Cardiff to Tonypandy, it seemed like a dream. The lad from the Rhondda was on the threshold of his greatest achievement. But like most dreams, it never materialised. George was never to become President of the NUT, for his life suddenly took a totally unexpected course.

George was still teaching at Roath Park School in early 1945. Although the classroom was the same as ever, a new elation still gripped him. The excitement of the Presidential election remained with him.

The war years had rolled by; with victory in Europe the city of Cardiff went crazy. People sang and danced in the streets; there were street parties for the children and suddenly the future began to look brighter. The excitment captured the children's imagination, particularly when they had a special day off school. Life was now seemingly on a steady course for George. A bachelor, he still lived at home with his mother in Tonypandy, and every morning he would catch the train down to Cardiff to teach. Much of the great poverty the Thomas family had known had sunk into the passing years, but George was still comparatively poor, and, like everyone else in those days of rationing, still had to find ways to make ends meet.

8

On to Westminster

Mrs Elizabeth Andrews JP was a remarkable lady. She was the first woman magistrate in South Wales, a person of vast energy and organising ability, and a Christian idealist. She had come into increasing contact with George through his involvement in the NUT and his membership of the Labour Party. Mrs Andrews had many commitments in public life, but one of her great concerns was the Labour Party in Wales. She had watched the virtual meteoric rise of the young man from the Rhondda, runner-up for president of the teachers' union at only 36, and Chairman of the Mid Rhondda Labour Party. Mrs Andrews knew he was in great demand as a speaker on political and social issues, and having heard George she knew why.

Mrs Andrews recognised the potential of the miner's son from the Rhondda, and in his idealism and Christian principles saw her own standards mirrored. Why shouldn't a man like George Thomas be in Parliament? Mrs Andrews decided to talk to George. A meeting was arranged and Mrs Andrews said, 'George, I've something I want to ask you. I would like to put your name forward for the panel of

Parliamentary candidates.'

George was silenced. Mrs Andrews went on to explain that this was a list of prospective candidates which went to all the constituencies in the country, to see if there was a candidate that a particular consituency would be interested in adopting. She also explained that putting his name forward, didn't guarantee his being placed on the list, or that any constituency would be interested; but she wanted to try.

This request was a bolt from the blue. Although taken aback, he was also profoundly grateful for the opportunity, and for the confidence Mrs Andrews showed in him. George discussed the matter fully with Mrs Andrews, and then said, 'Thank you Mrs Andrews; I'll let you have my answer very soon. I've got a lot to think about first.'

If George accepted the nomination, and was accepted by a constituency, he would have to give up teaching to fight the General Election. He loved teaching, and was well-liked by both the children and his colleagues. But it went further. He had been runner-up for President of the NUT and next year would be the President of the union; the pinnacle of his union career. If he agreed to Mrs Andrews' request, he would never become President. He had the opportunity of a possible new career, in politics; on the other hand with so much within his grasp in the union, should he now let it all go?

Mrs Andrews did not press George for an immediate answer. It was probably the greatest decision he would ever have to make, and she knew some of the personal choices that he had to resolve. She also knew he would not be pushed into something that he did not feel was right for him. They shook hands and George went to Cardiff Central Station to get the train home.

He was in a daze as he boarded the train for Tonypandy. As the engine puffed its way up the valley George stared unseeingly out of the window. A nagging doubt gnawed at his confidence. 'Who'll vote for me even if I am accepted?' Even his acceptance was uncertain, he was not yet on the list of Parliamentary candidates. Another anxiety was filling his mind, 'Even if I tell Mrs Andrews to go ahead, and they do agree to put my name on the list and suppose there is a constituency that adopts me as its candidate, and I fight the election – I could lose!'

The constituency could be at the other end of the country, far away from his beloved Wales. Would he have to go there to live? If he was to be successful, he would have to be closely involved in his constituency. If George was going to do a job, he would do it to the best of his ability – his mother had instilled that into him. He shook his head in bewilderment.

With these unresolved questions troubling him he went into the house and greeted his mother. George was very fond of his mother, deeply respected her opinions. She had come through many difficulties, but always maintained her radiant faith and shrewd understanding. He often talked over situations with her before making his decisions. George did not marry, and his mother remained his confidante until she died at the age of ninety-one. That evening she listened as George spoke with excitement and elation at the invitation to put his name forward, then downcast, said, 'Mam, what if I lost?'

Mrs Thomas had treasured a growing ambition for her son.' She wanted to see me in government and she did', George commented later. Now as they discussed the choice to be made, they remembered that nearly twenty years earlier she had said, 'George if God wants you to be a Methodist minister, doors will open. We will have to look for doors and we may have to push a little, but we will do our best.' Now a completely new opening faced George.

George loved and respected his mother, but his decisions

were always his own. His iron resolve to change social
conditions in the Rhondda valley and beyond was becoming tempered into a single purpose. 'I'll do it, Mam',
he said. The decision was made, and life was never the
same again. George went to see Mrs Andrews, and without
hesitation said, 'Now about the panel of Parliamentary
candidates, by all means put my name forward.'

George did not wait long. Quite soon he was asked to go
to Transport House in London for an interview. The man
who discussed his future and assessed this earnest miner's
son from the Rhondda, was Mr Shepherd, then National
Agent of the Labour Party and later Lord Shepherd. He
liked what he saw in George, whose name was added to the
long list of prospective candidates, which was circulated to
constituencies throughout the country together with brief
curricula vitae of the candidates.

It was difficult now for George to concentrate on his
teaching. Every day he would hurry home from Cardiff
and ask, 'Any post Mam?' Union matters still occupied a
lot of his time, and there was a lot of correspondence to
deal with; but still no invitation to stand as a Labour Party
candidate in the next General Election.

Eventually a letter with the postmark 'Blackburn,
Lancs' was delivered. George tore open the envelope: he
was requested to go to Blackburn to be interviewed by the
local management committe, with a view to being adopted
as one of the two Labour candidates for the next General
Election. Two candidates? George was puzzled until he
realised that Blackburn was a two member constituency,
and was to remain so until 1950. He was also intrigued.
'What will the other fellow be like? Will we get on together
alright?' He travelled to Blackburn and was surprised to
discover that the other candidate to be interviewed was in
fact a woman journalist, who had already made a name for
herself on the *Daily Mirror*. They immediately seemed to

get on well together. Barbara Betts was a vivacious young woman whose political ideals in many ways matched George's desires for social change. Barbara Betts, or as she is better known, Mrs Barbara Castle, later became a member of the Cabinet with George. Barbara Betts and George Thomas were both adopted as Labour candidates for Blackburn, and looked forward to fighting the Election campaign together.

Back in Roath Park School, Cardiff, George tried to concentrate on teaching. He was known as a kind man, but quite a strict teacher, and the children knew that if they had a problem Mr Thomas would listen with kindness. But they also knew that no one could take liberties with him. The afternoon wore on, broken only by 'playtime' for the children. George glanced up at the gas light in the class room which threw a pool of light immediately below them and left the rest of the room in darkness. 'I've got to do something about these lights', he resolved.

To the children it was just another afternoon. But George was preoccupied. His thoughts were far away and were a jumble of conflicting ideas. He had been asked to stand as a Labour Party candidate in the forthcoming General Election for a constituency in the north of England. It would mean great changes in his life, above all, leaving his beloved Wales, if he succeeded.

Down one side of the class room were windows separating it from the hall. George glanced out to see who was passing. The man walking down the hall may have been a stanger to everyone else, but George knew him well. George frowned, wondering why old 'Meth' Jones had come to see him, and in such an urgent manner. 'Meth' Jones was a retired miners' leader living in Cardiff. He was very active in the local Labour Party organisation, and much respected for his efforts. He and George had often met through their shared interests, and enjoyed talking together. As they had got to know each other better, George plucked up the courage to ask the question he longed to know the answer to. 'Mr Jones, er... well..er..why does everyone call you 'Meth?' His reply was surprising, 'That's my name.' Seeing George's amazement, he grinned and went on, 'I was christened Methuselah Jones, so folks call me, "Meth".' George burst out laughing. What optimistic parents to call him after the figure in the Bible who lived to be the oldest man. 'Meth' Jones and the young teacher remained good friends. It was not uncommon, particularly for those of 'Meth' Jones generation, to have Bible names. Even today in the valleys you meet men called Elijah, Seth, Zechariah, as well as Welsh names such as Idris, Ieuan and Islwyn.

Intrigued by 'Meth's' visit George greeted him. 'George', said the old miner, 'I've come to ask you something special. As you know there's a General Election coming, and I'm here to ask if you will stand for us as the Labour candidate for Cardiff Central.' He paused, waiting for an answer. George was taken aback. His name had already gone forward for a distant constituency, where he was a stranger and felt he hadn't too much chance of success. But this request – he would be standing in an area where he was well known, and would not have to leave Wales. It took his breath away.

After a few moments' silence, George asked, 'But Mr Jones, who will vote for me?' George genuinely wondered if he would have any real chance in the capital of Wales.

'Leave that to us, we'll see to it. Will you do it? Will you let your name go forward? We'll run the campaign, you'll see', 'Meth' Jones replied confidently and persuasively. George now found himself in a dilemma. A few weeks earlier he had seriously wondered if any local constituency would be interested in him. Now he had the choice of two!

The Thomas family
Back row, left to right – Ada, Mam Thomas, Dorothy (Dolly)
Front row, left to right – George, Emlyn, Ivor.

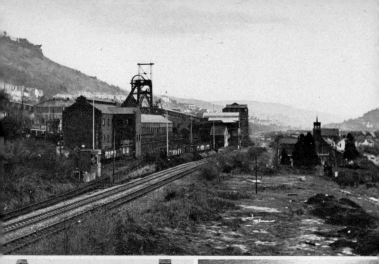

Top: A Rhondda Valley scene.

Lower left: The 'underhouse' where George Thomas spent his childhood. This was only the bottom storey shown in the photograph. The 'gully' with stone steps leading up the Miskin Road is now incorporated into the house, but where it was can be clearly seen to the right of the small window.

Lower right: George Thomas's coat of arms in the Speaker's House at the House of Commons.

Top: Trealaw Infants School where George Thomas started school.

Bottom: Miskin Road, Trealaw.

Top: The Methodist Central Hall, Tonypandy, where George Thomas regularly worshipped as a young man.

Bottom: Roath Park School, Cardiff, where George Thomas as a teacher was asked to stand as the Labour candidate for Cardiff Central.

Blackburn, a Lancashire town where he was a virtual unknown; his lilting Welsh accent betrayed him as coming from outside the area. George was determined that if he became a Member of Parliament, he would never be remote from his constituents. If he represented Blackburn – this would not be easy but he would do his best. On the other hand, Cardiff was so near; he knew the city, and was well-known because of his union involvement, and his Methodist local preaching. Here his rich Welsh accent was an advantage, for it marked him out as someone who understood Wales and the problems in the valleys.

So it had to be Cardiff Central. George shook 'Meth' Jones hand and agreed. George had to give up his teaching career to devote himself to the election campaign. The 1945 election was memorable for its six-week campaign. The dark years of the Second World War were past, but austerity remained; food was still rationed, and things were hard to get. But there was a great wave of idealism and hope that never again would Britain return to the hardships of the 1920's and 1930's. In the Welsh valleys there was a determination to build a better country. George Thomas said, 'We want a country in which mass unemployment will never return, and a society in which there will be no return of war.'

George now plunged into the turmoil of a political campaign. His name was on huge posters on the hoardings. 'Vote for George Thomas', they screamed at the passerby. But his political meetings were rather unusual; George saw to it that hymns were sung at every election meeting at which he was present. Whenever possible the minister of his local chapel in Tonypandy, the Revd Cyril Gwyer, was on the platform with him. Both in his speeches and answering questions, George made it clear that he was a Methodist local preacher and believed the Bible.

This was not only a crucial period in his political life,

6

but also in his personal life. Well-meaning friends suggested he should relinquish his preaching. 'It could put some people off', they said. George had to decide what he would do. His mind went back many years to his conversation with Owen Buckley in that street in the Rhondda on their way home from chapel in Treherbert. George knew he felt called to preach, and the more he thought about it, the more determined he became. He would continue preaching whatever the cost or opposition – and continue to preach he did.

Even with hymnsinging at meetings, not everyone got the message. When the final result of the ballot was announced, one man turned to old 'Meth' Jones and said, 'Duw, man, I didn't know that we were voting for a religious man, or I would never have voted for him.' 'Old 'Meth' Jones just kept quiet. George was later to comment 'The Lord must have kept him in darkness!' He has always been glad that from the beginning of his political career he made his religious convictions clear to all.

George had formidable opponents in the election. The Conservative candidate, Charles Hallinan, was a leading figure in Cardiff and was chairman of the Conservative Party in Wales. He was later to become Lord Mayor of Cardiff. George's other opponent in the election Peter Hopkin Morgan, was standing as the Liberal candidate and was younger than he was. He was a member of a great family of bakers known throughout South Wales.

In the election George seemed to be the 'under dog' with neither the experience nor the personal influence of his opponents. He fought his campaign on the basis of the slogan, 'No mother ought to suffer as mine has done.' He said this wherever he went, in public halls or at street corner meetings. To some, such a slogan may have sounded extremely naive, but it caught on; people in Cardiff began to realise that 'our George' (as they were starting to call him) knew what he was talking about, and understood their problems. This down-to-earth approach captured the imagination of many in the Cardiff Central Constituency.

George campaigned tirelessly. As often as she could Mrs Thomas was there too, helping in every way. Cathays, a densely populated area of Cardiff reminded George of his home in Tonypandy, with its small houses, tightly packed in long terraces, and with its similar closely-knit community.

Here on one occasion George was holding an open-air meeting, speaking into a microphone to a number of people who had stopped to listen. Women stood at the open doors of the neat houses, listening as George spoke of the needs of the area. There was an audible response as he shouted out his slogan. 'No mother ought to suffer as mine has done.' Others just walked past and ignored him, while some shouted back rival slogans. Suddenly a big man dressed in naval uniform elbowed his way through the listeners.

'Ere', he said 'give me that mike.' George looked up at the sailor; he was too big to argue with! George had no option but to let him use the microphone or possibly have a very ugly scene. So with trepidation, George handed him the microphone, wondering what he was going to say. The sailor took the microphone, glared round at the crowd, which had grown considerably, to subdue any possible challenge, and began to speak. What he said may have been a little rough but as he spoke, George relaxed, for he was putting over a fine speech on George's behalf. After a few minutes, the unknown sailor finished speaking and a ripple of applause ran across the meeting. He handed the microphone back to George, 'Thanks' he said, pushed his way through the crowd, and was gone. During the election campaign, George used this incident many times to illustrate how he felt he was speaking for the ordinary man in the street.

Of course, much of the campaign was routine; meeting after meeting, calling on constituents, listening to complaints, going from door to door, George enjoyed it all although it was very tiring too. He was to address an election meeting at the Canton High School, in Market Street, Cardiff. A young man in the audience stood up: 'I want to make a statement to this meeting', he said. 'I have something that I want to say.' The chairman interrupted him, 'Please sit down. You can ask a question later, but you are not making any statement here.' Every eye fastened on the young man, who remained standing. Suddenly George's eyes widened in surprise, then, turning quickly to the chairman, he said, 'Let him speak. Let's hear what he has to say. If necessary, I'll answer him.' As George had stared at the young man, he had recognised him. His memory had taken him back to that morning in school more than ten years earlier, when a thin-faced little boy had fainted into a little heap on the classroom floor because of hunger. The young man standing in the audience that night was that boy.

'Alright.' said the chairman, who knew nothing of the young man's life, 'Mr Thomas says you may speak.'

A strange hush came over that school hall as he told simply what had happened. How as a child he had been deprived, and could not even afford to have his little bottle of milk. He spoke with emotion of George Thomas's kindness; 'He saw to it that I always had my milk after that.' He sat down, and for a moment there was complete silence. Here and there people wiped away tears that had come to their eyes as the story was told so simply. George Thomas says, 'You know, his speech was far more effective than any of mine.'

The 1945 election was also unusual in another respect

too; following a campaign lasting six weeks, there was a delay. The Parliamentary candidates had to wait five weeks for the count and declaration of results. The delay was because in 1945, Great Britain still had more than two million men and women serving in the forces overseas. They were in all parts of the world, and it was rightly thought that they should be able to cast their votes in this election, when Britain was rebuilding after the devastation of the war. Arrangements had been made for them to cast their votes wherever they were serving. The votes were then sealed and sent back to Britain for counting.

Votes were cast in steamy jungles of Burma, in the deserts of North Africa and in the formerly Nazi occupied countries of Europe. British people in Cardiff and Cologne, Reading and Rangoon put their cross on the ballot paper to choose a postwar government. It would take five weeks to make sure that all the votes had reached their correct destination. On the night of the official count, the votes from overseas were tipped out of their boxes together with the local votes and the counting could begin.

As a candidate, George was present for the count. Experienced electioneers told him it was possible to get a rough idea how things were going by looking at the votes as they were counted. As the hours passed, George's excitement diminished. He looked at the piles of ballot papers and every one he saw seemed to have the cross on the top line not on the bottom line where his name appeared. George became despondent.

Friends and helpers from his local Party kept coming to him. 'George, it looks as if you're in,' said one. Another shook his hand, 'Congratulations George, the way things are going it seems that you've won.' George couldn't believe it. He went to look again as the count went on; still every paper had the cross opposite the name of his Conservative opponent. He thought his friends were simply trying to encourage him, but George was certain that the Conservative had gained the victory.

After all, Winston Churchill had come to Cardiff to give the Conservative Candidate his personal support. George knew that tens of thousands of people had lined the streets of Cardiff to cheer the great war-time leader. Surely they must have voted for the candidate he supported.

George was lost in thought as he travelled back up the Rhondda Valley to Tonypandy. The public declaration of the results was to be the next day at Cardiff's City Hall. Whilst disappointment gripped him, George was determined he would accept defeat gracefully. When he arrived home, his mother and stepfather asked, 'Well George, how is it going?' Glumly, George answered, 'Everyone says that it looks as if I'm elected, but I don't believe it, because it looked to me as if the Conservative is in.'

George's mother had planned to travel to Cardiff for the declaration of the results. 'Mam, now don't you burst into tears when they announce that I'm defeated. That would be terrible. Remember, we must take it well.' His mother, now getting on in years, still had that iron resolution that had taken her through so many difficulties. 'Don't you worry, George,' she assured him. 'I won't let you down. You can count on that.'

Next morning, when George looked through his bedroom window, he saw that the skies were like lead, and torrential rain was beating on the Tonypandy pavements. George still felt despondent, but he knew that he must be present at the declaration of the election results. It would be courteous as well as customary to offer his congratulations to the Conservative Candidate, whom he was sure had won. As he walked to the station through the rain the day matched his mood – grey and sombre.

Arriving in Cardiff he made his way to the City Hall. Just outside this white stone building, impressive in its setting in Cathays Park, George met his Conservative opponent.

Crowds had already begun to gather, braving the torrential rain to hear the declaration of the results. George Thomas and Charles Hallinan greeted each other warmly. They were political opponents not enemies. George Thomas holds no animosity to those who have opposed him even if they did so at times with angry speeches. As Speaker he has many friends on both sides of the House of Commons. He says, 'It's a very narrow minded fellow who bases friendships only on Party affiliation.'

The Conservative candidate and the Labour candidate shook the rain from their coats and walked up the wide staircase in the City Hall. George, convinced that his opponent had won, said generously, 'Well Charles, you are in and I congratulate you.' Charles Hallinan thanked George for his kind congratulations. He had not been present at the count the previous evening, and so had not been able to assess the result.

However as the two men entered the City Hall to go to the Lord Mayor's Parlour, George was suddenly bewildered. 'Well done, George', someone shouted. Another said, 'Congratulations, George, you're in', people tried to shake his hand. George felt shaky as it dawned on him that he had won the seat and was now a Member of Parliament. He looked around for a chair – he just wanted to sit down for a moment, as he was so surprised. In the Lord Mayor's Parlour, amid the congratulations, George's eyes searched among the many people there. He questioned officials passing to and fro. His anxiety grew. Where was his mother? He wanted her to be here with him in this moment of triumph. She had struggled in poverty, taught him the great truths of the Christian faith and inspired him by her own example as an untiring Party member. This moment of victory was hers as well as his.

With the other candidates, George went outside with the Lord Mayor for the announcement of the results for the Cardiff constituencies. He stood there in his old long raincoat as the results were announced. The pouring rain did not dampen the enthusiasms of the crowd; a loud cheer rang out as the number of votes cast for Charles Hallinan was announced; another cheer when the total was given for Peter Hopkin Morgan. Then the Lord Mayor announced, 'Thomas George Thomas, Labour,' and the number of votes was drowned in the roar of delight as the crowd realised that he had won. 'Our George' had done it. He was going to Parliament.

Standing by the Lord Mayor's side as the announcements were made, George was still searching for his mother. Suddenly he saw her. She was in the crowd waving excitedly with hundreds of others. The rain was pouring down and she was getting soaked; but she was there and George felt proud.

After the declaration of George's constituency's results, the Lord Mayor announced Hilary Marquand elected for Cardiff North. George offered his congratulations to him and then turned to greet the newly-elected member for Cardiff South. They shook hands warmly and congratulated each other not realising how distinguished their careers were to be, as Speaker of the House of Commons and Prime Minister. George Thomas and Jim Callaghan began a long friendship and working relationship that day.

Years later, when Jim Callaghan became Prime Minister, the *Guardian* published a photograph of that scene in the pouring rain. Someone looked at the photograph with George standing in his long raincoat with the collar turned up, 'You looked poor in those days, George.' George grinned and replied, 'Well I was poor, and that's the truth of it.'

9

Life on the Back Benches

George's excitement in gaining a seat as an MP increased as he realised that Labour had won a landslide victory. He entered Parliament with 399 other Labour MPs, including Jim Callaghan and Michael Foot. He could hardly wait for his first day in the House.

The election resulted in a dramatic victory for the Labour Party. Altogether 399 Labour MPs were returned, giving them a clear majority of 146 over all other parties. The Conservatives had to take the blame for the Munich agreement, and for the failure to rearm, as well as for pre-war unemployment. There was also a good deal of concern lest the post-war situation should resemble that after the First World War, when the lavish promises of Lloyd George had led to very little fulfilment.

Trade-union sponsored Labour MPs now numbered less than a third of the total; there was a flood of young middle-class MPs, many of them professional men – lawyers, journalists, teachers, doctors, dons. About two-thirds of the Labour members had never been in Parliament before. The first day in the chamber was crowded, for there are not enough places to seat all the members. Such an arrangement may seem inadequate, but it preserves the conversational concept of the House. The first matter was the election of the Speaker. George felt he was taking part in history. It was very cramped; sitting between Jim Callaghan and Michael Foot, George hoped he would not catch Michael Foot's cold.

George turned to speak to Foot, 'I am a great admirer of your father, Isaac Foot. He is a great man.' Michael Foot knew of George's Christian faith and replied, 'Yes my father is a good man but I don't share his religious convictions.' George Thomas believes that the Christian has a special contribution to make in politics: 'Our starting-point is surely just where Jesus began. He dealt with men in their daily work and made it abundantly clear that his teaching applied to their relationships with each other. No one has a better opportunity of touching men's lives in this way than the modern politician. With the growth of State influence and the development of welfare services, politics are brought right into the homes and workshops of the land. Almost everything that happens to modern man is influenced by politics. Even when he falls in love and seeks to build his home he soon finds that the State wields mighty power over his activities.

'Clearly, the quality of the contribution made by people caught up in politics depends on the basic faith they hold. If their beliefs are limited to Party loyalties, the contribution will be small. Everything will then be measured in the petty perspective of Party advantage.

'What is essential in politics. . . is a recognition that even Parliament's powers are limited when it comes to the provision of society's most vital needs.... The cornerstone of good government is good people. Not all the legislation in the world can make a bad man good: legislation based on even the highest ideals is useless until men accept its moral standards.

'The problem of modern politics is not a want of planning or of legislation. It is the want of spiritual insight and Christian values. We are suffering the consequences of a massive abandonment of Christian worship. Realization of this is now beginning to spread.'

Clifton-Brown, Conservative member for Hexham, was re-elected to the office of Speaker which he had fulfilled admirably. Later, it became known that when Clifton-Brown heard of the Labour landslide victory, he went to the Speaker's House and packed his personal belongings ready to move out. He thought that the Labour Government would not re-elect him, a Conservative. However the Labour Party led by Clem Attlee respected the traditions of the House and there was no difficulty in re-electing Clifton-Brown.

The newly-elected MPs had to wait two or three days before they could take their oath personally. George went forward to the table in the centre of the Chamber, and taking the Bible in his right hand, repeated the oath in a firm voice. 'I swear by Almighty God that I will be faithful and bear true allegiance to King George VI, his heirs and successors according to law, so help me God.' He then moved on a few yards and fully sensing the occasion, signed the book. A few more steps, and George was introduced to the Speaker, who greeted him saying, 'Welcome to the House.'

About three hundred new members entered the House in 1945, and each wanted to make his maiden speech as soon as possible. Only three days after the King's speech for the new Parliament, George made his debut. But his first speech did not have an auspicious beginning. Other MPs who wanted to speak were standing, and so was George. Mr Speaker, Clifton-Brown called out, 'Mr Roberts' and everyone sat down. The Speaker pointed at

George and said again, 'Mr Roberts.' George stood up and said, 'I am George Thomas, sir', and then the Speaker announced him correctly.

His first speech was on a theme that George was to continue for the next twenty-five years. He felt passionately about the need for leasehold reform. He had seen so much hardship and heartache in Wales because of problems relating to leasehold property, that George was determined to see changes that would stamp out abuses of the system.

The new member for Cardiff Central soon gained a reputation as a hard-working MP who cared about people. Every week he ran a 'surgery' where people could come and explain their problems, and he would do his best to help. He had few resources so he began holding his 'surgery' in a private house in Romilly Road, Canton. There were so many wanting to see him that often there was a long queue of people waiting, and George would be there five or six hours without a break. Obviously he had to make other arrangements. 'Even the carpets started to get worn out with all those people, so I took pity on my friends and moved out.'

The next venue for George's surgery was a small hall in Cowbridge Road, the main road leading into the city from the West. The hall was owned by two local men, A. J. Williams, later Lord Mayor of the City, and another councillor, John Higginbottom, who had moved there from Oldham.

As George listened to peoples' problems he soon discovered that most were to do with housing. With many young men coming back from the war and many newly-married people, squatting was a great problem. Young men returning from years at war were used to taking drastic action, so they simply moved into empty buildings. As the weeks went by following his election to

Parliament, George decided to specialise in leasehold reform. Everytime he held a 'surgery' he was sure to encounter someone in distress, about to lose their home because the lease had run out. Sometimes people also faced a bill of hundreds of pounds from the ground landlord, who had the right to insist that the house be put into good condition before it was handed back. 'Mr Thomas', people asked bitterly, 'What can we do?' It was a problem particularly prevalent in Wales.

George knew the problems of leasehold from his own experience. Some people living in a house in Cathays, staunch supporters of George, had wanted to help him in his election campaign. They invited George to use the front room of their terrace house as a committee room. Regretfully, and with some embarrassment, they then had to tell him that he couldn't use their front room. The ground landlord told them that if they allowed George to use the room, they would be breaking the conditions in the lease and he could turn them out. Angry, George vowed that he would do his utmost to change things.

A procession of people had been to see him in the little hall in Cowbridge Road. Their requests varied; some were trivial, others needed immediate attention. Then two old ladies came in ill at ease and upset. George motioned them to sit down. 'Tell me what I can do for you?' he asked gently. Through their tears, these two frightened old ladies told their story. As George listened, consuming anger enveloped him. The two women were spinsters. They had spent their lives looking after their parents, until they had died at advanced age. The house had been left to these two daughters, but the lease was running out, and the ground landlord had sent them a bill for £400 for repairs to the house. He was pressing for payment. 'Mr Thomas, what can we do? Where can we go? We can't pay all that.' They were frightened out of their wits.

George comforted them as best he could and promised to help. With unswerving determination he went to see the ground landlord. After talking for a while without apparent success, George said, 'They haven't got the money and therefore they can't give it to you. If you take legal action we'll have the whole community against you. You'll lose a lot of money in legal fees, too, because they can't pay costs either.' George glared at him angrily. The ground landlord hurriedly decided to waive his claim, but the old ladies had to pay rent for staying in the house their father had bought for them. George comments. 'It was a cruel system. The small print in some of these leases would have done Shylock credit!'

From that day, George Thomas became totally dedicated to a change in the leasehold system. He campaigned not only in his first Parliament, in which he failed to get the Labour Party to do anything, but continued until the government of Harold Wilson in the 1960s. As a member of the Cabinet, and as a direct result of his pressure the Leasehold Reform Bill was introduced, giving people the right to buy the freehold of their homes at a reasonable and fair price. If a landlord did not make what appeared to be a reasonable offer it could go to arbitration to fix a fair price. With deep satisfaction, George Thomas says, 'of all the things that I have taken part in whilst in Parliament, the greatest joy that has been given to me was the Leasehold Reform Bill.' Overnight, more than a million people found that they could buy the freehold of their own homes. When this Bill became law, George still did not own a home of his own; later he was also to benefit from this act of Parliament when he became a home-owner.

George campaigned tirelessly for the needy. He wrote regularly in the local paper and was called 'George Thomas champion of the underdog.' He can never forget the hardships of his own early life, and it continually spurs him on to do what he can for the needy.

A few months after being sworn in, George met Anthony Eden, who asked, 'How are you settling in, Tommy?' (Eden always called him Tommy.) 'I love it here, Mr Eden', was George's reply, 'there are some marvellous people in this place aren't there?' It may have sounded a little naive, but George was sincere. Anthony Eden looked at the new MP, and smiling wrily said, 'Yes, there are some of the others too. The great thing is that you choose your own friends. You be careful Tommy, choose the right ones', and walked on down the corridor. George watched his tall figure moving away and realised what good advice it was.

It seemed an eternity since George had been teaching in Roath Park School, as so much had happened to him in the last few months. The excitement of the election campaign, the thrill of the announcement at the City Hall, his confusion when as a newcomer to the House finding his way around, and getting to know its traditions. But something hadn't changed – those gas lights in Roath Park School! George remembered how they gave merely a circle of light on the desks immediately below leaving the rest of the classroom in darkness. Now was his opportunity to get something done. When his opportunity came, George stood and addressed his question to the Minister of Education in the Attlee government, Ellen Wilkinson. he asked at considerable length what she was going to do to replace the gas lights in Roath Park School. George was warming to his subject, and going on rather a long time. A shout came from the Opposition benches. Sir Walter Smithers, Conservative member for Orpington, called out, 'Too much gas!' The House dissolved into laughter, no doubt, increased by George's pronounced Welsh accent. He still laughs at the memory, 'If you think I have a Welsh accent now, let me tell you I sound like an old Etonian now when compared to my accent then.' He realised one must be able to laugh at oneself and not take offence in the House of Commons.

The Government decided to propose National Service, that is peacetime conscription. To some MPs this proposal was abhorrent, and George was one of them. As a pacifist, he felt that he could not vote with his Party on this. George is a patriot but peacetime conscription stirred his conscience.

It was a difficult time for him as he made his intentions clear to all. George was an extremely loyal Labour Member, but could not support this proposal. Matters came to a head when a three-line Whip was imposed on Labour Members. A three-line Whip is the ultimate in compulsion; each member must be present and vote according to Party policy. If an MP is at the other end of the country, he has to be in the division lobbies when the vote is taken. But George refused. Clem Attlee called a meeting at which George and others who felt as he did, had to be present! The meeting was held in Room 14, the scene of much political drama, George remembers. 'It certainly was a famous room, for there Nye Bevan was expelled from time to time from the Labour Party.'

As George made his way to Room 14, his mind was in a turmoil. He was at the beginning of his political career, and yet in rebellion against a three-line Whip. Perhaps this would be the end of his political life. During the meeting, Attlee was severe with George and the others with similar views.

George waited for an opportunity to speak. Finally he stood to put his point of view firmly, concluding with words that were to be remembered for a long time, 'Mr Attlee, I am sorry to tell you that even if there was a 43-line Whip I cannot and will not vote against my conscience.'

The matter had to rest there. In some quarters, it made George unpopular, but it also stamped him out as a man of integrity. Even political opponents gave grudging admiration to this young man with convictions as solid as rock.

Of course being new to the House George was not very well known. A few months later he discovered that Winston Churchill was to visit Cardiff to receive the freedom of the city. George would be present as one of the Cardiff MPs but as yet had not had an opportunity to speak to Churchill. 'What a terrible thing if he didn't know who I was', George thought. With this in mind, the day before Mr Churchill was to visit Cardiff, George went looking for him, feeling the humblest of backbenchers. He found the great man in the Smoke Room of the House, surrounded by a group of friends.

George paused for a moment, and then said, 'Please excuse me gentlemen.' Mr Churchill looked up at George inquiringly. 'Mr Churchill', George continued, 'You are coming to the city of Cardiff tomorrow to receive the Freedom of our city, and we are looking forward to seeing you. My name is George Thomas and I'm the Member for Cardiff Central.' Winston Churchill gave a grunt, smiled and said, 'Yes and I consider it a great honour that you are giving me. I look forward to it.' George repeated his name. 'Well, I'll see you there, sir, oh, and my name is George Thomas.' Mr Churchill smiled again and George went away pleased and relieved.

The next day Mr Churchill arrived in Cardiff. Thousands of people turned out to cheer him. The crowds remembered his inspiring leadership during the war. Churchill, the Lord Mayor of Cardiff, and about a half-dozen others, including George, sat taking coffee and chatting together. During a lull in the conversation in the Lord Mayor's Parlour, Churchill turned to the Lord

Mayor, motioning towards George with his famous cigar said in a loud voice, 'Who's that over there?' much to George's embarrassment.

Recalling the incident George says. 'Do you know I never found out whether he had really completely forgotten me or whether he was enjoying a leg-pull, remembering his own days as a young backbencher.'

George would not be subdued on matters about which he felt strongly, although it was his first Parliament. There was a great battle on a matter which some Members considered trivial, but which to George was a matter of principle. Should Battersea Park Fair be open on Sundays? Herbert Morrison, former Leader of the London County Council was Leader of the House. He favoured the fair being open on Sundays. Together with some other Welsh Members and Scottish Members, George bitterly opposed it. The whole idea went against his Methodist upbringing. George stood in the Chamber, and when called, launched into an angry speech. 'Maybe my honourable friend', addressing himself to Herbert Morrison, 'has been often described as a little Englander, because he doesn't know much about foreign affairs, and his horizons are not very wide. Mr Speaker, he is not a little Englander – he's a little Londoner and his boundary doesn't go beyond London. London may want it but they must remember the influence of the rest of the country.' Then George sat down. There were angry scenes because then the Sunday question was of great significance; and men like George were prepared to speak out concerning their Christian view point.

Sitting in his office reliving that debate today, George Thomas comments, 'Perhaps I was a little cruel in what I said to him, but I believed passionately in those matters then, and my Christian faith is as strong now as ever.'

George believes that the Christian enters into a great tradition of political reform: 'Politics without the refining influence of Christian teaching is a jungle of competing interests. It is the State that grows and the individual who shrinks in all political activities that ignore the Christian belief that man is a child of God. Democracy cannot last on any basis other than a spiritual one, for it is more than a political system where majority opinion decies all policy. It is a way of life based on faith in the ability of people to respond to high ideals. Democracy accepts the fact that human personality has possibilities that the social system dare not impede. It is an attempt to give political inter-pretation to the philosophy embodied in the words 'Inasmuch as ye have done it unto one of the least of these my brethren ye have done it unto me.'

'For the Christian realises that wherever there is social injustice or exploitation the will of God is being defied. The State exists to add to the dignity of man, but neither to control him nor to diminish him.

'Because bad social conditions serve to cramp and cripple the personality of the workers, Christians have led the way in a demand for Parliamentary action right down through the years. Every great political reform in British history that has added to the rights of man has been inspired by Christian activities.' *The Christian Heritage*.

The method of voting in the House of Commons is called division. When a vote is announced, MPs leave the Chamber and have eight minutes to reach the division lobbies, at the southern end for those in favour and at the northern end for those against. As MPs leave the division lobbies, passing the desks where the count is taken, each member is noted on the list, and an accurate count is obtained. George found that first Parliament exciting, and on many occasions, when walking through the division lobby, he and other Welsh MPs would sing. As they were in the lobby, a voice would call out 'Come on George', the cue to start singing. George and the Welsh MPs always sang the Welsh tune *Cwm Rhondda* to which the words are, 'Guide me oh thou Great Jehovah.' George sang as heartily in the division lobby as he did in the Central Hall in Tonypandy, and thought nothing strange of it.

In 1946, George spoke in the debate of RA Butler's Education Bill: 'It is far more important in my opinion that a child should receive a good education in a stone building. I happen to live in the Rhondda Valley and I am a son of a Rhondda Valley. I welcome that part of the Bill which gives to the Education Authority power to clothe a child....'

As a back-bencher, George felt totally fulfilled. He had no burning ambitions for high office, but was determined to be a good constituency member, caring especially for those he represented. The people of Cardiff Central had put their trust in him; George would not let them down. In twenty years as a back-bencher, he concentrated almost solely on questions relating to problems in his constitency, and to issues affecting the people of Wales.

In 1948, George's stepfather, Tommy P.D. died. Since all the children had left home except George, it meant that when George was in London, his mother was alone in the house in Tonypandy. They therefore decided to move down the valley to Cardiff. His mother still an ardent Labour Party worker, although getting on in years, could become involved in his Cardiff constituency work. Travelling back to and from London would also be more convenient for George.

It was a great wrench for George and his mother to leave the Rhondda valley. The valley, the towns of Trealaw and Tonypandy, the chapels; all with poignant memories for them both. There had been great hardships, poverty and family and personal crises, but it was here that George had grown up.

During the 1950s there was a proposal to open cinemas

and public houses in Wales on Sunday. In Cardiff, George led the campaign against what he thought was a desecration of Sunday as the Lord's Day. Church leaders had come asking him to lead the campaign, and although many of his friends thought he was making a mistake, George would not be deterred; it was a matter of conscience. Some of his local Party workers felt his involvement could wreck his chances of re-election and asked him to withdraw. But George Thomas, practising Christian and Methodist local-preacher, was not persuaded by that argument either.

His involvement was raised in the local management committee of the Labour Party. One young man proposed a motion that George be asked to stop leading the campaign. Whilst he was speaking, George, usually very polite interrupted him. 'Let me save you a lot of time and trouble. If you are going to try and muzzle me on matters of conscience, I don't want to stand for Parliament again. So you can choose somebody else whom you like.' He sat down in silence. After a few seconds, the meeting moved on to other matters, realising George was adamant in his beliefs.

George's campaign was not successful. When the results of the voting on this issue in Wales were known, Cardiff had the biggest defeat! It had been an unpopular stand and George had been deluged by letters and post-cards opposing him. Some of them were unpleasant and others threatening. Yet George was not deterred by threats; he had the courage to stand by his convictions.

When the next election came, George did not lose votes, as some had feared but on the contrary greatly increased his majority. He comments: 'I think they liked the fact that I was willing to stand on my own if necessary, if it was something in which I believed.' However public support for the Labour Party started to ebb. The next election began to loom ominously before George. Not that he was

afraid of going back to the people, for he had done his best
for his constituents. But a new and unpredictable situation
could influence whether he would be re-elected.

In 1950, it was decided to revise constituency bound-
aries. The seat held by George, Cardiff Central, would
become Cardiff West. George had won the trust and
affection of his constituents, and now he was to lose forty
per cent of them in the boundary changes. He would have
to campaign in areas of the city which were new to him,
and he wondered if this might cost him the election. He
was determined to campaign more vigorously than ever.
The thought of defeat must be put out of his mind.

In 1950 he held his seat, although the Labour Party's
majority was drastically cut. 'You know', he says today,
'when you think about it, I've represented sixty per cent of
those in my constituency for thirty five years, that's a
complete generation.'

During an education debate in 1950, George drew on
his personal experience as a teacher: 'What are the qualities
we look for in the teacher of today? I believe that he
requires the patience of a Job, the courage of a Daniel, and
the wisdom of a Solomon and the understanding of a saint,
for which he shall receive the reward of a beggar.…
Teaching is a vocation that calls for sacrifice, but there is
no need for the community to feel that needless sacrifices
should be imposed upon them!' The general election of
February 1950 had given the Labour Party an overall
Commons majority of only six, and this created a
Parliamentary situation that made government almost
impossible. It was quite out of the question to attempt any
contentious legislation, and the ordinary needs of administration could only be satisfied by great strain upon both
ministers and MPs – for, however busy or ill they were,
they had to attend all important divisions of the House to
save the government from defeat. To the fury of the

Conservatives, the government let iron and steel national-
isation take effect in 1951.

Faced with the heavy cost of rearmament, Hugh
Gaitskell put charges on glasses and false teeth available
under the Health Service. This provoked the resignations
of Aneuran Bevan, Harold Wilson and John Freeman; but
the government continued to lose popularity. With the
index of prices still rising, Attlee called another election.

The General Election was called in 1951. A Conservative
Government was elected and quite a number of George's
colleagues lost their seats. Although it was a defeat for the
Labour Party, it was a personal triumph for George.
Against the tide of popular opinion, George actually
increased his majority in Cardiff West. Some in positions
of influence soon took note that the Member for Cardiff
West, was not only an idealist, but had good understanding
of Parliamentary procedure. This coupled with his
exuberant humour, gained him many friends on both
sides of the House. He was a formidable opponent in
debate, and could say some harsh things but he never
carried that outside the House. He saw all as his friends –
they might see things differently from him but that was no
reason to bear animosity. George has proved by experience
that Parliament has a place for the Member with a
conscience.

'A major fear preventing Christians from involvement
in Party politics is that when a clash of loyalties occurs they
will not be able to follow the dictates of their own
conscience.... Party discipline is seen as an impediment
to a full Christian witness. With an unflattering readiness
to believe the worst about politicians, it is assumed that
when a clash occurs expediency triumphs every time. This
is sheer escapism. People who are only too glad to have an
excuse for not bestirring themselves and to avoid becoming
involved in a wordy battle accept it readily. Neutralism is

unworthy of Christians.

'It is no harder for a man to express his Christian heritage in the House of Commons than it is for a man in the factory, whether at shop steward level or in the company chairman's office. In politics, as in industry and commerce nothing prevents a determined man from expressing himself freely and proclaiming his convictions for all to hear.

'Ever since Simon De Montfort's skeleton Parliament in 1265, the voice of Christian believers has been raised at Westminister demanding measures of social justice and reform. They have done so with no greater strain on their conscience than men in other walks of life. There is a sense in which it is easier for politicians to follow conscience than it is for any other worker. Every political party has its conscience clause, which enables Members to abstain from voting on an issue in which the party offends against their conscience.

'Common experience proves that the conscience clause covers every issue raised in Parliament. No Member of Parliament who has genuine and deeply felt religious conviction which prevent his supporting his party in the division lobby need ever fear recriminatory action by the party cabal. It is when the convictions are so powerful that the Member feels impelled to vote against his party colleagues that disciplinary action follows.

'Toleration of people with opposing views is a Parliamentary heritage in these islands. Day after day issues of principle arise and personal crises are revealed as votes are taken.

'Of course, because familiarity breeds contempt there are always some folk willing to jettison any principles that hinder success: but this is not a politician's weakness; it is a world-wide affliction amongst ambitions people.' *(The Christian Heritage)*

In 1953, Sunday observance came up for discussion. George played a full part in the debate: 'I happen to believe that Christianity is the corner stone of democracy; that its emphasis on the value of the individual, on the rights and responsibilites of men is all-important in the fashioning of our way of life. After all, it is the Christian faith that has given to the world a lively concern for the sick, the poor, the oppressed and the down-trodden....

'In Holland I understand that this day is spoken of as God's Dyke. Just as their dykes protect their low-lying land from the on-rushing waters, so Sunday protects the working people of the land from the on-rushing tides of materialism, commercialism and exploitation in general.'

George had already gained a reputation as a man of integrity. He could not please everyone by the stands he took, and would take in the future, on matters of conscience: but neither would he be hypocritical. These qualities led to an invitation to serve as a Chairman of Standing Committees in the House of Commons in 1950, an office in which he continued until 1963. It meant that from time to time George had to chair the Committee of the whole House. These early days were the preparation for the success that George Thomas has been as Speaker of the House.

In 1959 George was one of four Labour candidates who were aided by the National Union of Teachers during their election campaigning. With the country on the verge of the General Election of 1964, Bert Bowden, Chief Whip sent for George. 'Come in George', said Bowden. 'As you know, there'll soon be the election and if we win, you are to become Deputy Speaker and Leader of Ways and Means.' George listened in amazement. This meant George would be a Privy Councillor, giving him the title of Right Honourable George Thomas. At times, too he would have to act as chairman of the House. Technically, the members of the Privy Council are advisors to the monarch: in practice only those serving in the government are called on to advise.

George left the office of the Chief Whip almost walking on air with excitment. Yet there was an election to win. Some of the newspaper polls predicted that Labour would lose, whilst others predicted a very narrow win. Once again, George plunged into the election campaign, spurred on by the thought of what he would become if Labour won. When the results were declared, George had been re-elected with a large majority and Labour had again won the election.

10

Climbing the Ladder

Labour won the election but the majority was less than had been hoped for, George began to feel uneasy about the promise that he was to become Deputy Speaker. He prepared himself for disappointment. This was no new experience; he had known much disappointment in his life from his childhood poverty to student struggles.

On the Sunday after the election, the phone rang. As he picked up the receiver he discovered it was to ask him to meet the Prime Minister next morning at Number 10. For the rest of the day George wondered why he was to see the Prime Minister.

A number of people were standing outside when George arrived at Number 10 anxious to discover who the new Cabinet were to be. George hurried in, anxious to know if he was Deputy Speaker. Harold Wilson began to explain to George that he could not be the Deputy Speaker. The Prime Minister spelled out the reason, which was purely political. George had all the qualities ncessary to be the Deputy Speaker but the Labour Party held a majority of only five seats. If George became the Deputy Speaker, he would be unable to cast a vote in the House, except when there was a tied vote. It was essential that George remain in a position in which he could vote in the division lobbies.

George said little, as he tried to conceal his disappointment. He was a loyal Party man, and what was best for the Party was what mattered. He would get on with his job and do the best he could for his Party and his Cardiff constituents. Then Wilson said, 'George, instead I am offering you the post of Parliamentary Undersecretary of State in the Home Office.' This was a new and exciting challenge; and since the Home Office is one of the oldest departments of state, it would broaden his understanding of government. The two men clasped hands as George accepted the position, and the Prime Minister wished him success in his new post.

George found the Home Office very different from what he had expected or been led to believe. Commenting on the first week in his new appointment, he says, 'The Home Office had a reputation of being stuffy and stodgy, but I was not there a week before I realised that this was a very unfair description.'

He was surprised at the responsibility he was given; he was to be responsible for Sunday observance, drinking and licensing, gambling, the police and the general department, which covered everything that no other department could take responsibility for. 'Imagine, me a teetotal, Methodist preacher in charge of all those matters!' was his comment.

The Prime Minister came into the Members' Tea Room on one occasion soon after George had assumed his new responsibilities, and walked over to where George was sitting with friends. 'What's this I hear about you George?' he asked. 'I hear you are responsible for Sunday observance, drink and gambling, now you are in the Home Office.' 'Yes Prime Minister, that is correct; that is my job', he replied. Harold Wilson raised his hands in an expression of horror. 'We are in enough trouble as it is, George, without having you with your views looking after all that!'

The Carlisle Brewing Industry had been in public ownership since the time of David Lloyd George. It was necessary to call a conference of the brewers from Carlisle, and George, as the Undersecretary had to preside. The representatives from Carlisle arrived in London, and the meeting commenced in the Home Office. Opening the meeting, George welcomed the Conference and then said, 'Well gentlemen, I never thought I would be presiding over a meeting of brewers, with the personal views I hold!' Suddenly there was an interruption, 'Excuse me, Undersecretary, we are not the brewers. It is you who is the brewer!' There was a roar of laughter, in which George joined as much as anyone. For years after George was teased unmercifully that he had become a brewer – a teetotal brewer – in the interests of the government.

Of course there were also difficult days for George in the Home Office, as he confronted some of the great problems of our society. He dealt with immigration too, and saw much heartache in bewildered immigrants. As Undersecretary he had to handle the most difficult cases, which he attemped to do with compassion and understanding, but never with weakness or by seeking an easy way out.

He recognised that there had to be restrictions. 'I have always felt that these small islands cannot take all the population who want to flock here. We have to have a limit on the number simply for housing, education and the social services.' But George also made it clear that the door was open for those who were fleeing from persecution, or seeking to rejoin their family. Some cases he found it very difficult to deal with. There were those who had borrowed money to come to this country, and would be sending instalments back for almost a lifetime. Sometimes the immigrants had been cheated out of everything they possessed by unscrupulous agents, who promised to arrange everything. Such matters gave George insight into the problems of other countries. For most of George's time at the Home Office his superior was Sir Frank Soskice, with whom he had a happy and co-operative relationship. Soskice was willing for George to state his views strongly, as he was so inclined himself. However for George's last six weeks at the Home Office his senior was Roy Jenkins. Roy Jenkins held very different views on society from George. One day, as the two were talking, Jenkins began referring to a speech of George's about gambling. George regards gambling as a social evil and a curse to those who are enmeshed by it.

'George', said Roy Jenkins, 'If you are prepared to say nothing further about gambling, then I promise I'll not talk about Sunday observance or the drink question.' They looked at each other for a moment, then George just laughed. Roy Jenkins understood without a further word. George would not be silenced on matters of conscience.

Whether by coincidence or design, within two weeks George was promoted away from Roy Jenkins. From time to time, a conference was held to decide whether men serving life sentences for murder were eligible for parole. In one case there was a difficult decision for the Secretary of State to make. The medical advice was that, if a man was not released after ten or twelve years, he could become a human cabbage, devoid of personality. This had to be weighed against the likelihood that he would again resort to terrible violence; the public interest had to be taken into account. George found this discussion moving and disturbing. He was involved in deciding a man's future, and felt the weight of that responsibility, although he would not be making the final decision.

With his reputation as a politician growing with a remarkable insight into people's problems, George served in the Home Office until 1966. Perhaps his greatest quality was integrity; people knew they could trust George Thomas – not only his friends but political opponents too.

1966 was another election year and George, campaigned as forcefully as ever. Although he was now climbing the ladder of success he never forgot his responsibility to his constituents. George may have been Parliamentary Undersecretary at the Home Office, but to the people in Cardiff he was still 'Our George.'

George held street meetings, campaigned in school halls in his constituency and when the polls closed for the 1966 election, he felt confident. His confidence was not misplaced; George Thomas was re-elected with a still greater majority.

The general election of 1966 had given the Wilson government a good deal more than the ample parliamentary majority that it required for a normal term of office. It also increased the authority of the Prime Minister, since it was apparently his personal qualities, in comparison with those of Edward Heath, the new leader of the Tories, that won the government its confidence vote.

The trade-union group was weaker than before; only six of the 65 new MPs were traditional trade union men. Over half the Labour MPs now were graduates; there was new talent on the Labour benches.

After any election there are bound to be changes in the Government. George did not know if he would return to his responsibilities in the Home Office, or in fact if he would be given any office. In the event the Prime Minister asked George to become Minister of State in the Welsh Office. The Welsh Office then was not large, and the Secretary of State was a great personal friend of George's, Cledwyn Hugh, MP for Anglesey. The two men worked well together and George's period of the Welsh office was most enjoyable. He was able to travel throughout Wales and discovered much about his own land. Of course George was still deeply concerned about social conditions in the South Wales valleys, and did all he could to promote Welsh affairs.

George Thomas played an important part in the events following the appalling disaster at Aberfan in October 1966 when a tip collapsed on part of this Welsh mining village. Harold Wilson graphically recounted the affair:
'We were driven one and a half – or two – miles back up the main road, then turned right across the valley and into the road immediately below the road where the houses and school were. We could only get half way along because of vehicles, and walked the rest through thick squelching black mud, varying an inch to three inches in depth. We then turned left to where the houses were – what looked like a smoking heap of matchboard, bric-a-brac and mud, no one could have told there had been houses there at all. Men were digging and machines were scooping mud away under the searchlights. We then went down back along the road and turned up the path – which as we all felt was probably the path where the children had gone to school that morning – and then along to the school where we scrambled up the slope through all the workers, diggers, baulks of wood being carried and even banging into us. A number of the workers came up, shook hands and some of the bereaved parents just came and shook hands saying nothing.
'The school hall where we went was open to the sky. And then half way along it was a great heap of black mud rising higher than the roof would have been and then merging with the pit heap itself. On the wall where we were standing were children's drawings, safety posters etc. . . .
'George Thomas was perhaps the most effected as he had

·taken on the job of comforting the relatives and had attended the meeting of relatives held by the Director of Education.

'On the Tuesday afternoon George Thomas, who had by this time returned to London and who was still pretty moved and shattered, told me of the reaction of some of the people to the visitors. They were obviously glad that I had gone – but the highest praise was for Lord Snowdon. He had gone spontaneously and, instead of inspecting the site, had made it his job to visit bereaved relatives. George Thomas told me of the things he did – sitting holding the hands of a distraught father, sitting with the head of a mother on his shoulder for half an hour in silence. In another house he comforted an older couple who had lost 13 grandchildren – in another where they were terribly upset he offered to made a cup to tea....'

About a year after his appointment to the Welsh Office, George was in Cardiff for an official dinner. George was guest of honour at a dinner connected with St. David's Hospital, one of Cardiff's oldest hospitals.

George was called away to take an important phone call. 'It's from the Prime Minister, Mr Thomas', said the messenger. As George listened to the Prime Minister, his eyes widened in surprise, then he thanked the Prime Minister, and returned to his seat as guest of honour at the dinner. The Prime Minister had offered George a new position that would take him further afield than Wales. He had been asked to become Minister of State in the Commonwealth office. Although it was a wrench to leave the Welsh Office, concerned with affairs so close to home, the new position presented a field of opportunity and experience. George had accepted the post, knowing it would involve him in world travel and meeting heads of Commonwealth countries.

As Minister of State, George soon plunged into the

many activities that his office demanded. Some were pleasant and involved him in representing the government at events in the Commonwealth countries. He was delighted to go to the coronation in Brunei, for example. Other matters called for careful diplomacy, and some for resolute determination. George presided over a meeting of the High Commissioners from all the Commonwealth countries who berated Britain for not making sanctions against Rhodesia more effective.

One of the sad episodes of George Thomas' career involved his visit to Nigeria. Civil war was looming. He went to meet both factions to try to find a solution, but the divisions were too deep, and within hours of George's arrival in the country, the war broke out. The Military Officer in charge of Nigerian affairs was Jack Gowan, a religious man. Before they spoke together, he insisted on a prayer and a Bible reading. Of course this did not embarrass George but the civil servants who had accompanied him were 'a bit put out.'

George returned to London and in subsequent months was tempted to resign, he could not justify the supplying of arms to one side in the civil war. He tried to rationalise his position. Finally, after much heartsearching, he came to the conclusion that if he resigned, it would suggest that a pacifist had no place in modern government. George would never opt out of any responsibility, yet recognised he had to work with colleagues holding different viewpoints. 'I believe that there is plenty of room in government for people with strong convictions that might not be the convictions of their colleagues.'

There were growing problems in Uganda, and Ugandan soldiers had been beating up Europeans. Anyone travelling along a particular lonely road was stopped, forced to get out of their car, and beaten. Britain had been making strong protests through diplomatic channels to Dr Milton Obote,

President of Uganda, but to no effect. Finally the acting British Commissioner made a public speech about the beatings and the British protest. Dr Obote was furious, particularly as he was having his own difficulties with the military, although the British were not fully aware of this. George was in charge at the Commonweath office since it was August, and the Secretary of State at the Commonwealth Office was away on holiday. There was such a diplomatic uproar in Uganda that George was advised to recall the Commissioner for consultations. This he did, but this was only the beginning of the problems which landed on George's shoulders. Dr Obote was so angry that he refused to allow the British Commissioner back into Uganda. This created a major diplomatic problem and an urgent meeting was called by the Prime Minister at 10 Downing Street. The matter was fully discussed and finally the Prime Minister said, 'Well there's only one thing for it, the Minister of State will have to go out to Uganda to see Dr Obote and settle this matter.'

George had been given negotiating terms that if the Commissioner was allowed back for a month, the British Government would move him quietly to another appoint-ment. Face-saving is important in political life; and George realised that he had a delicate situation on his hands.

He met Dr Obote and his Cabinet at State House Kampala. It was very hot and the meeting was held outside in the open air. For six hours George negotiated with Milton Obote, without success. George remembers him playing with his stick, making circles on the ground as they talked. George had asked the Commissioner be allowed back for two months, to give himself a little leeway in negotiation. But it was to no avail Dr Obote continued drawing circles in the dust with his stick, and flatly refused to have the Commissioner back.

George was equally determined; so there was deadlock.

Finally George stood up, looked at Dr Obote, and said severely, 'Very well, the Commissioner WILL come back next Wednesday afternoon. 'Dr Obote was startled; 'But I've said no, he can't return.' But George was insistent, the iron resolve beneath his natural charm, had come to the surface. 'He is returning next Wednesday, 'George said. 'You have accepted his credentials as High Commissioner, and if you stop him coming, it will be world news and there will be trouble for you.' There was a hurried consultation and Dr Obote decided to adjourn the meeting, saying that he would see George again the next morning. But George was unmoved. 'I am leaving for Kenya tomorrow, and if you wish to try and stop the British High Commissioner whose accreditation has been accepted by you, then the responsibility is yours', and George left the meeting.

Dr Obote met George Thomas next morning before he left for Kenya, and again face-saving was important. Dr Obote said, 'I can't agree to his returning for two months but I will agree to one month.' George's face remained expressionless; 'No Dr Obote, not one month, but I will meet you half way. We'll say six weeks.' They agreed and the two men shook hands. What could have been a long diplomatic quarrel had been settled honourably and without loss of face.

There had been hard words spoken and fierce arguments in negotiation, but privately the two men remained on friendly terms. One evening Dr Obote gave a State Dinner in George's honour. It was a fabulous evening and the guests were entertained by traditional Ugandan dancing. At this dinner George was introduced by Dr Obote, to the Chief of Staff, a huge man whose build dwarfed the slight figure of George Thomas. They shook hands and said a few words after which George turned to others in the queue of people waiting to talk to the representative of the British Government. Quietly Dr Obote gestured towards his big Chief of Staff, 'He's called Amin and I know that he is after my job, but I'm one step ahead of him and I'll keep there.' In private, George told Obote that he thought it a mistake to replace all the white people in the armed forces, but the president disagreed; a coup could not happen in Uganda. Less than a year later when he was in Singapore, the government was overthrown and General Amin took over with the ensuing bloodshed and atrocities.

This successful diplomatic mission to Uganda greatly enhanced George's reputation as a negotiating representative of the British Government, and when another problem arose in Africa George was again asked to go to sort it out.

The focus of attention this time was in West Africa. General Ankrah had taken over in Ghana, and was demanding the extradition of a former Ghanaian High Commissioner who had remained in London. General Ankrah and his colleagues alleged that this man was guilty of corruption and must be returned to Ghana to face trial. It appeared there were political overtones to this demand. Roy Jenkins, the Home Secretary, objected strongly to any idea of extradition, because it is a principle of this country that if people will suffer for political reasons, they should not be sent back to their own country. We have a long tradition of giving refuge to people fleeing political persecution.

This led to a fierce quarrel between Britain and Ghana. Harold Wilson, the Prime Minister, said, 'I think the Minister of State should go out to Ghana and try to settle this matter.'

On this mission George's negotiating terms were not impressive. He was to negotiate with General Ankrah that the man accused of corruption would go on trial in London and the world would hear the impartial verdict. Britain would always be a refuge for the politically oppressed, but not a haven for the criminal. He would go on public trial.

With these as his only bargaining counters, George went to meet the General. It was initially a most unpleasant occasion. The General was fuming with almost uncontrollable anger, and as soon as they met launched into a tirade of abuse. 'I had heard of man's eyes bulging, but I had never seen it in my life before. I didn't believe that it was anything more than just a descriptive phrase. But I give you my word that this man's eyes seemed as if they were going to pop out of his head. He was gifted at finding new abusive adjectives for almost every sentence he used.'

This torrent of invective continued for almost half-an-hour and it seemed as if George would get nowhere on this mission. As General Ankrah paused momentarily George angrily interrupted, 'Have you quite finished, General?' But the irony was lost. 'No, I have not', he replied, and carried on abusing everything British.

The problem was how to convince General Ankrah that when George gave his word that the man at the centre of this storm would go on trial in London, he meant it, and the British Government meant it. To make the General understand that George's word was his bond, he began by saying, 'General, I am a Methodist...' General Ankrah interrupted 'What...you say you are a Methodist?' George nodded. 'Put it there', the General said, holding out his right hand. George took it and they shook hands. The officials of both delegations were visibly relieved and the temperature quickly cooled. Within a few minutes the matter was settled on George's terms, as prescribed by the British Cabinet.

The reason for this sudden change was that Methodism had been very widespread in Ghana during General Ankrah's youth, and he had come under its influence.

Although he was not a practising Methodist, General Ankrah still had great respect for the Methodist church. George had inadvertently touched a great influence in General Ankrah's early life, and so succeeded in a delicate mission.

His period at the Commonwealth Office was one of the most interesting in George Thomas' life. He travelled widely and his influence and integrity became ever more respected. He visited Pakistan and India and was shown some of the temples and the exquisite stone carvings. Some of the temples are more than 4,000 years old; one that fascinated him was built so that it was covered by the sea at high tide, and could only be visited at low tide.

However George was not there as a sightseer but to represent the Government. Such interludes were a pleasant part of the diplomatic round, but his real purpose was to meet Commonwealth heads of State. It was on this visit to Pakistan and India that George learned forcibly that it is always best to be frank.

After a little time in Pakistan, he went to India to meet Mrs Gandhi. George thought it would be tactful not to mention his visit to Pakistan, particularly in view of the animosity that existed between the Pakistani and Indian Governments. George and Mrs Gandhi talked for some time about political problems concerning the Commonwealth and especially India, and finally they exchanged presents. As they did so Mrs Gandhi looked at George and with a smile said, 'How did you get on last week in Pakistan, Mr Thomas?' George was taken aback that she knew about his visit. 'Well, Mrs Gandhi, I found them to be lovely people, they are hardworking people and I cannot speak too highly of them.' He then waited for some sharp words from Mrs Gandhi, but was surprised when she replied, 'Of course they are lovely people. They are our people and we are their people. They should never have broken off for those religious reasons. In any case, we have more Muslims in India than they have in Pakistan.'

He learned that day that it was vital to be straight-forward even when the guest of a Head of State.

These and countless other experiences broadend George's mind. As a young man, he had been pre-occupied with the problems of Wales; as he progressed in public office, he became more aware of the problems of the entire British Isles. Now at the Commonwealth Office he became aware of world situations. The horizons of the Rhondda valley had given way to a world view.

Richard Crossman's notorious diaries show something of George's principled stands during his time at the Commonwealth Office. He relates how on Monday March 11th, 1968:

'The row started with the Sunday Entertainments Bill where, as usual, we had decided to declare neutrality but wanted to give time for a House of Commons decision. Now here we had a really formidable small pressure group – the non-conformist Welsh teetotalers – who strongly objected to our giving even neutral support to the Bill. So George Thomas came to the Cabinet and demanded the right to speak against Sunday opening even though he has nothing to do with the Home Office and just wanted to express his views as a lay preacher. Thomas was sur-prisingly supported by Jim Callaghan who asked why, if on the Abortion Bill Roy Jenkins is allowed to give positive arguments in favour of abortion, George Thomas shouldn't speak against this?'

Crossman also reported George's courageous opposition to restrictions on the immigration of Kenyan Asians in the same year:

'Whitehall had lined up the DEA, the Ministry of Labour, the Ministry of Education, all the Departments concerned, including even the Foreign Office, behind the Home Office demand that the law must be changed. Only the Commonwealth Department stood out against this pressure and George Thomas, the Minister of State, made a most passionate objection to the Bill in strictly rational form, saying this was being railroaded through and Jim was getting backing from all the Departments!'

Although George was at the Commonwealth Office for a comparatively short time while there he saw the end of an era. During the period there, the Commonweath Office was merged with the Foreign Office, indicating that the country was beginning to look away from the Commonwealth and towards Europe.

Yet again the Prime Minister sent for George to offer him a new position. Now Harold Wilson asked him to return to a greatly expanded Welsh Office, as the Secretary of State for Wales. This meant that George would become a Privy Councillor and a member of the Inner Cabinet, the small team of ministers with whom the Prime Minister talks over major issues before going to the full Cabinet.

George was thrilled to be involved in the Welsh affairs again. However he did not long remain a member of the Inner Cabinet. Dick Crossman and George Brown complained that there were others senior to George. However, undismayed, George continued to serve as Secretary of State for Wales.

There was an event looming on the horizon that would tax all George's political ingenuity, but give him perhaps his greatest opportunity to express his love for Wales. When Harold Wilson offered the new post to George, he said, 'You realise don't you George, that you'll be in charge of the Investiture of Prince Charles next year.'

11

Land of my Fathers

When George Thomas returned to the Welsh office as Secretary of State, it was the beginning of a turbulent period in Wales. The Investiture of Prince Charles as Prince of Wales was just one year away, and Welsh Nationalists were seeking to build up hostility to the Investiture. In the House of Commons, Gwynfor Evans, the Welsh Nationalist MP for Carmarthen, was asking hostile questions and some Labour members argued that it was not right to spend £200,000 on the ceremonial for the Investiture.

Things became increasingly difficult for George as the Investiture drew nearer. Extremists tried to enforce their view by violence and over fifty bombs exploded throughout Wales, damaging pipelines, roads and public buildings. One such target was within George's own domain, the Welsh Office in Cardiff, damaged by an explosion.

George felt this deeply, since he has a personal love for his own land, and was doing a great deal to promote the Welsh language. George is not the most fluent of Welsh speakers, but during his period as Secretary of State he arranged for more money to be spent on preserving the Welsh language than ever before. No one could be more patriotic than George.

George's predecessor in the Welsh Office was Cledwyn Hughes who advised that Prince Charles should spend a few weeks at Aberystwyth University College before the Investiture. This would make the Welsh people feel that the Royal Family and Prince Charles in particular were acknowledging Wales as a cultural and national entity.

Prince Charles was placed in part of the University where he would be surrounded by Welsh-speaking people. Although eight out of ten people in Wales speak only English, the authorities at Aberystwyth felt Prince Charles should be with the keenest Welsh speakers, and he was in fact given a Welsh Nationalist as a tutor. This could have been difficult for the Prince, but he soon learned some Welsh, and became very popular, enjoying much of student life at Aberystwyth. He was happy in Aberystwyth and grew to such an appreciation of Wales that Prince Charles makes more visits to the Principality than any other member of the Royal Family.

George had always been convinced that the people of Wales would turn out in their thousands to greet the Prince, and prove to the world that the extremists were a tiny minority. Events proved him absolutely correct.

Of course many other tasks confronted George at the Welsh Office. During this period the Welsh Office continued to expand, and responsibility for the National Health Service in Wales was placed under its jurisdiction. Other responsibilities that passed to the Welsh Office included agriculture in Wales and all the castles in Wales. George Thomas comments. 'When we lost the election in 1970 I lost 200 castles overnight.'

There is no doubt however that the greatest task that George Thomas faced as Secretary of State, was to ensure

the smooth running and success of the Investiture. He
tried to foresee every contingency, and the people of Wales
responded magnificently, especially those in the little
town of Caernarvon, North Wales, where the Investiture
would take place in the great castle. This quiet holiday
centre suddenly became the focus of world attention.

As the day drew nearer, preparations were feverishly
made. The town was decorated and thousands of people
began to arrive. A new station was built to receive the royal
train, and arrangements were made for the Royal Family
to drive by carriage to Caernarvon Castle, a partially-
ruined fortress which dominated the town. Newspaper
reporters, photographers, television and radio personnel
thronged the narrow streets for the historic event. Scores
of police and security men were brought in, though everyone hoped their presence would prove to be unnecessary.

Not everyone wanted to be involved, and at one point, it
appeared that George himself would not be able to attend.
On the day of the Investiture, Gwynfor Evans, the Welsh
Nationalist MP obtained permission for an adjournment
debate in the House of Commons, objecting to the
Investiture, and arguing that the money should be spent
on the old age pensioners. This was a ploy to prevent the
Welsh Office minister attending the Investiture, since he
would have had to remain in London to answer the debate
for the Government. In the event George asked another
Government minister, Judith Hart, to answer for the
Government and so was able to go to Caernarvon.

George was determined to ensure that the Investiture
ceremony would be appreciated by the men and women of
Wales. While planning the event, George had met with the
Investiture Committee and discussed the music for the
Investiture. The song, 'God bless the Prince of Wales' had
been dismissed by a figure of considerable standing as
poor music, and not worthy of this great occasion. George

was incensed, and fought hard to have the song included. 'Well, I don't know about the music,' he stated forcibly, 'I haven't been trained and educated in it, but I know I like it, and I know the Welsh people like it.' George looked around the table and continued, 'you would be very foolish not to have this song.' His strong words carried the majority of the committee and 'God bless the Prince of Wales', was included in the programme.

On the Sunday before the Investiture, George travelled to Caernarvon to see for himself the preparations for this once-in-a-lifetime event. It was a sunny day and the windows of his car were open. The town was packed with people, and there was a very happy atmosphere. George's car moved very slowly indeed. Suddenly, as the car was forced to stop by the crowds of people, two men in their early twenties pushed their heads in through the open windows and spat out one Welsh word into George's face, 'Bradwr' (traitor). George was shocked, because in this happy and excited crowd, the incident was so unexpected. He quickly regained his composure and to the surprise of the two men, said in Welsh, 'No, it's you who are the traitors.' They glared at him for an instant and then disappeared into the crowds. It was a tense moment because there was nothing to prevent them dropping an explosive device into the car.

Shaken by the vehemence and hatred of the men, George had to make a quick decision. He could have the car windows closed, a strong police guard and wave remotely to the crowd from his car. With scarcely an hesitation George decided on the opposite course of action. As the car began to move again, he ordered, 'Stop the car, I'm getting out.' The excited crowds gave a great cheer when they saw that the Secretary of State was getting out. George walked among them shaking anonymous hands thrust out to him in welcome. He was detemined to let the people see he was not afraid, and would not be deterred from his task. There was no sign of the two young extremists, and George was given a tumultous reception. He was visibly moved at the affection of the people of Wales.

The day in 1969 when the Investiture took place is a day George will never forget. Even before daylight crowds were gathering in the streets, securing the best places to see the procession to the castle. As the time drew nearer every window was curtained by excited faces peering down on the crowds beneath. Across the country and beyond, people watched the scenes on television.

For George Thomas there was the privilege of going to the special station to greet the Queen and to escort Prince Charles to Caernarvon Castle.

There was some initial delay because the special train had been held up for two hours when signal wires on the line were cut. It was a great moment as George the miner's son from the Rhondda, greeted Queen Elizabeth II. The Queen asked George if anything had happened during the night. It was with some reluctance that George informed her that during the night two men had blown themselves up whilst attempting to place a bomb by the side of the railway line. He felt it deeply that a minority was trying to bring violence to this great occasion in the land he loved. But George went on to reassure the Queen, 'You are going to receive a great welcome, I've just come from the town, and it's crowded with people. The people are so excited that they were even cheering me! I know you'll receive a marvellous welcome.'

Prince Charles was the first of the Royal family to leave the train and drive to the castle. The Prince and his equerry, together with George, were escorted to the open carriage that was to take them through the streets of Caernarvon. As this magnificent carriage set off Prince Charles looked across at George. 'Mr Thomas, do you know that this is the coach that was used by Queen Victoria?' To which George replied, 'Well sir, I hope she was more comfortable than I am.' The Prince grinned understandingly; the seats were very narrow. 'It was the most uncomfortable ride I have ever had', George said remembering the occasion.

They had only travelled a short distance when there was a thunderous explosion. A bomb had exploded only half-a-mile away. 'What's that Mr Thomas?' asked Prince Charles. George determined that this day would not be marred in any way if he could help it, replied, 'Oh, that's a royal salute, Prince Charles.' The Prince looked at George quizzically, 'That's a peculiar royal salute', to which George replied, 'We're peculiar people up here, sir.' They grinned at each other as the horses pulled the swaying carriage into the town.

As Prince Charles passed through the narrow streets of Caernarvon the welcome was tremendous. Ringing cheers drowned any extremist dissent. Wales was receiving her Prince. Perhaps the most emotional moment for George came as the carriage reached Caernarvon Castle; the whole crowd, suddenly began to sing, spontaneously, 'God bless the Prince of Wales.' George eyes became misty, for this was the song he had fought for in the Investiture Committee. It didn't matter whether the music was of the highest quality; the Welsh were welcoming their Prince with their song.

The setting for the Investiture was magnificent. The Queen sat on a circular platform and a little to her left stood George Thomas. The platform was in the middle of the beautiful lawn, surrounded by the huge ramparts of this ancient fortress, which had witnessed so much pageantry through the centuries.

Following the Investiture, Prince Charles made a tour of Wales, passing through the towns and villages of north and mid Wales to the capital city of Cardiff. The welcome of Wales reached its crescendo in Cardiff, as tens of thousands of people poured into the city, many travelling down the valleys from the mining towns.

At the end of the week of the Investiture, Prince Charles gave a party on Saturday night on board the Royal Yacht, berthed in Cardiff docks. Dockers cheered and cheered as the Prince arrived at the Royal Yacht. George Thomas still glows with pride as he remembers the dockers' welcome.

Prince Charles' party is memorable for George because his mother, now well into her eighties was also invited. She had often travelled in George's official car during his period as Secretary of State, and George never forgot how much she had sacrificed for him. He did his utmost to care for her, and now when public office meant his being away a great deal, George made sure a housekeeper was always present to look after her. At Prince Charles' party the eyes of mother and son met; they had come a long way since the 'underhouse' in Miskin Road, with its three tiny rooms. In that look was the memory of his mother sewing for a pittance to try to provide for the family, and George as a student looking at his two and sixpence pocket money.

As the evening drew to a close, Prince Charles told George he wanted to give him a souvenir, and presented him with a signed photograph. 'Thank you, Prince Charles', said George warmly, and his irrepressible humour surfaced, 'I'll put it where we look the most in our house, on top of the television.' In fact that portrait, with another signed photo of Prince Charles, now stands in the Speaker's House at the House of Commons. George went home that night with his mother satisfied at how the Investiture plans had gone so smoothly. But more than that, he was thrilled at the warm welcome the people of Wales had given to Prince Charles.

It was a turning point in Welsh history. The welcome had shown that the extremist minority who are prepared to resort to violence had no support. Never again could it be said that the Welsh nation did not want a Prince of Wales.

George continued to serve in the Welsh Office until the 1970 election. Despite his concern for the affairs of Wales as a whole he never lost touch with his constituents. 'Our George' made sure he had time for the people of Cardiff West.

It had not taken more than a few months for the Prime Minister and the government to lose all favour in public opinion. By early 1967 the Tories had pulled ahead in the opinion polls. There were serious divisions inside the Cabinet, and in 1968 and 1969 despair was expressed by some of Labour's loyal supporters. By-election swings against Labour reached 20 per cent in 1968, although by May 1970 Labour had recovered to show a slight lead in the opinion polls. Wilson decided to try to renew his mandate on the strength of this and called an election. George flung himself into the election campaign with as much vigour on his first election campaign 25 years earlier. He was certain that the Labour Party would be returned to government; all the predictions showed that the Labour Party would win the election.

The people of Cardiff West re-elected George with a resounding majority. He looked forward to continuing as Secretary of State for Wales, and was determined to pursue Welsh Affairs vigorously. But as the results began to come in from all over the country, George became uneasy. As he watched the television reports, it became obvious that Labour was losing ground. The unpredictable had happened; the Labour Party lost and a Conservative government, under the leadership of Edward Heath, was elected.

9

Suddenly George was out of a job. It was hard to believe, and still more difficult to accept. Less that a year before he had been involved in the triumph of the Investiture, yet now he was just another Member of Parliament in Opposition.

When Parliament reassembled, George felt strange sitting on the Opposition benches, on the Speaker's left-hand side. Harold Wilson, now leader of the Opposition soon asked George to be Shadow Secretary of State of Wales, so that he would still be involved in Welsh affairs, travelling throughout Wales putting forward the Labour Party's viewpoint.

George viewed his new opposite number with interest and respect. The Secretary of State for Wales in the Conservative Government was Peter Thomas, who came from North Wales and was bilingual, being a fluent Welsh speaker. Peter Thomas and George were good friends both having the interests of Wales at heart, even if their policies differed. George describes Peter Thomas as 'a very delightful and charming fellow', although they had fierce battles in debate.

The next four years were very demanding for George. As Shadow Secretary of State, he did not have civil servants to research material, prepare speeches and check on facts. As George was always conscientious, it involved a great deal of hard work for him and he missed the help to which he became accustomed as a Government minister. He did his utmost to ensure that Labour's viewpoint on Welsh affairs was well presented but George also felt much frustration in Opposition.

There is no doubt that George Thomas's strong convictions owe much to the the teaching and example of his mother. Both George and his mother were teetotal, and it was only when Mam was eighty, that on doctor's advice, George persuaded her to take a drop of whisky before going to sleep. Although she was now quite frail she had adamantly refused previously. It was now known as 'Mam's medicine.' Once when she was eighty-nine, the frail old lady looked at George as he sat with his arm around her, and the tiny glass was brought in, 'George, I hope I don't get too fond of this stuff.' Her son laughed, and replied, 'I don't think it will ruin you Mam!'

George was utterly devoted to his mother, and not having married, was at home with her in Cardiff as often as he could. He loved to have her ride with him in his car when travelling as Secretary of State for Wales.

He was almost shattered by grief when on 21st April 1972 she died. She had been taken to hospital only the day before. About a month after the funeral, George was shaving and as he looked into the mirror he felt utterly alone. He felt that he had no one, and dark depression settled on him. He had maintained a living Christian faith through the years that had stood many tests. At his mother's funeral, the minister had spoken of the Christian hope, and George had found much comfort in accepting that she was now with her Lord. But that morning devastating doubts almost crushed him. 'What if it wasn't true? What if he had been fooling himself and there would never be a reunion.' Tears filled his eyes as he thought of his family, now gone.

He felt so alone. He thought of his eldest sister Ada, who had married and borne six children. She had lived in Peterston-super-Ely, a village near Cardiff, but at the age of 42 had been knocked off her bicycle and killed. Then there was Dorothy, dear vivacious Dolly, who was striken with tuberculosis and died at 56.

Picking up an old photo he looked at his older brother Emrys, who had gone down the pit at thirteen, his tiny wages helping George to stay on at school. After years of suffering, trying to catch his breath as his lungs were destroyed by coal dust, he developed cancer of the stomach and died at 56. Now 'Mam' was gone. The only other remaining member of the family was George's younger brother, Ivor, who was desperately ill in hospital. Ivor had struggled with ill health for nine years and died within a month of this sudden crisis that gripped George. With a heavy heart, George finished shaving and sat down to think and pray but nothing seemed to work. He was determined to hold on to his Christian faith at any cost.

He confided this deep struggle to no one and continued his constituency work and as Shadow Secretary of State. He tried to remain the same friendly, witty George Thomas but it was hard.

Describing his deepest feelings, he says, 'I thought to myself of all the people through the ages who had held onto their faith, and who had believed, as I believed, in the resurrection of our Lord. I said to myself, 'I believe, I want to believe, I'm going to believe.'

This personal struggle lasted for two weeks; two weeks of torment for George. Then the darkness and depression lifted, and the light of a vital Christian faith came back. Never again would the weight of such doubts and fears threaten to crush him. George's Christian faith had been tested and had come through stronger than ever.

George still regards Christianity as a revolutionary creed: 'It overturns and undermines everything else when once it becomes a guiding principle. Men fear it because of its revolutionary content. It provides such new measurements for success and such new bases for relationships that they have been reluctant to commit themselves to it.

'Primacy of love for God and man is the characteristic of every real Christian witness. This is the acid test of sincerity. It is the beginning and ending of all the Christian heritage in politics. By this yardstick we measure every policy and programme, for only when love decides our attitude is our programme even likely to be right. Christianity's tradition is the welfare of the needy. Just as Jesus identified himself with social outcasts, with misfits and with people whose only fault was in their poverty, so must we make such identification in our public witness. The need of men is the need of God so far as we are concerned. We serve Him when we serve them. This is the only way in which we can surmount the disappointments and betrayals of those we serve. This the true greatness for Christians that by the practice of Jesus' ethic of love we make ourselves the servants of all.

'It is as we accept the responsibility of being our brother's keepers that we make Christ's witness in the world.

'There is no doubt at all about this. This is love in action. It enhances the dignity of the individual and gives to his service a tone and quality that could not possibly be obtained in any other way.

'For the Christian compulsion is to respect human personality. No policy that offends against that complusion is open to the disciple of Jesus, who believed in winning the loyalty and allegiance of His followers: never to bully or browbeat them into accepting the truth of His teaching. Indeed Jesus sought to capture men by respecting them and loving them. That loyalty which was gained through legality or compulsion was not worth having: it would only last until the compulsion disappeared. His entire ministry rested on the conviction that the only way to serve men and to recognize their inherent value was through love.'

Early in 1974, the country was in industrial turmoil and a General Election was held. Local Party workers rallied round and George travelled from meeting to meeting in Cardiff, speaking on the vital issues. Still popular in his constituency, people stopped him in the street to wish him success. Young people, who had not even been born when George first entered Parliament, promised him their vote and affectionately referred to him as 'Our George.' He was moved by the support of a new generation of voters, who had never known another MP in their constituency.

When the campaigning was over, George waited confidently for the results. This time his confidence was not misplaced. He was returned to Parliament with a substantial majority, and the Labour Party returned to power. George waited expectantly to hear from the Prime Minister that he would return to the Welsh Office. He had enjoyed the department, and had now spent nearly seven years as either Secretary or Shadow Secretary.

But Harold Wilson asked George to become Deputy Speaker and Chairman of Ways and Means, the office promised to him ten years before. At first George was extremely reluctant. He wanted to return to the job he knew and the office he enjoyed although to be the Deputy Speaker would be a great honour. However, since Ministers cannot pick and choose their positions, George accepted.

When George first became Deputy Speaker, he found it difficult to get used to. For twenty-nine years George Thomas had been a loyal Labour party MP. His speeches whether from the back benches, the Opposition benches, or as a government minister, had been Party policy speeches, except for those few occasions when his conscience was in conflict with policy. Now, as Deputy Speaker, he was suddenly thrust outside the party political battlefield, and was no longer making Party speeches. He felt his loyalty was now to the House of Commons, rather than the Labour Party, to which he had belonged since his early days in the teaching profession.

It was a moving experience for George to receive the freedom of his home town. He was made a Freeman of the Borough of Rhondda. Cheers rang out; the Rhondda valley was still home to George Thomas. As he rode through the familiar streets, George could not help recalling the past. He had played in these streets as a little boy with patched trousers. Almost every town in the Rhondda held poignant memories. Treherbert where one Sunday night, old Owen Buckley had said, 'You should be a preacher George.'

The gas lights had gone from the streets; cars lined some of the streets where he had played as a boy. No longer do coal-blackened miners file through the streets. Pithead baths have taken care of that. The Judges' Hall, Trealaw, where George made his transforming decision about the Christian faith as a lad of sixteen, is now a venue for Bingo, and sadly the Methodist Central Hall has been closed down.

Thoughtfully George looked through the window of his car as they travelled through the valley. Many of the tips that had towered like black pyramids have been cleared; others have been landscaped. Grass and trees have been planted; a transformation is taking place.

New housing projects have placed modern brick houses among the old stone-built houses, and on top of the mountain above Trealaw a housing project has changed the skyline. Even the house in Miskin Road has changed. The 'underhouse' where George grew up is now part of the main house, and the old gully, down which he used to run from Miskin Road has been incorporated into the house, forming the stairs to a basement. Only the uneven stone steps worn by the passage of uncountable feet are unchanged.

George looked from the changes of the valley to the unalterable friendliness of the people. These are his people, his friends, the warmth of their welcome made him glow with pleasure. He had travelled the world, but to be a Freeman of his own home valley was a culminating joy.

The other great honour was when in 1975, with Jim Callaghan, George was made a Freeman of the city of

Cardiff. The only regret George had of the occasion was that his mother could not be present since she had died three years previously. As Foreign Secretary, Jim Callaghan had the privilege of taking Henry Kissinger as his guest to the ceremony. George talked at length with Dr Kissinger and was surprised to find him different from his public image of a cold and remote man. 'I found Henry Kissinger a much warmer personality than his public image leads us to believe. He was a warm and friendly person.' In his speech, George said he felt God had used Dr Kissinger to help bring peace to the world, and was surprised to see him moved almost to tears. George treasures the honour of being a Freeman of Cardiff, because without a break he had represented the people of Cardiff for thirty years.

George served as Deputy Speaker of the House for two-and-a-half years gaining a wealth of experience, as he observed the Speaker of the House in action, and at times took the Chair himself. Dick Crossman had introduced a reform concerning the Speaker's office. When a Speaker retired, he should do so during the life of a Parliament rather than at a General Election. This would avoid the problem of the House being faced with both a new Speaker and a new Parliament, and would give the opportunity for parties represented in the Commons to meet and decide whom they wished to nominate as Speaker.

When George served as Deputy Speaker, Selwyn Lloyd was Speaker of the House. Although the two came from opposite sides of the House, Selwyn Lloyd being from the Conservative Party, they had a happy working relationship each now giving loyalty to the whole House.

But after two-and-a-half years, Selwyn Lloyd told George he intended to retire, and was about to give ten days notice, as required by Dick Crossman's rule. George realised that, as Deputy Speaker, he had a chance of becoming the new Speaker. He did not build his hopes up too high, for he had known disappointment before. And there was another new factor. For the first time, Parliament could discuss who they wanted as the new Speaker. Would the Scottish Nationalists or Ulster Unionists even think of him. How would the Liberals react? Who would the Conservatives suggest?

12

Mr Speaker

The office of Speaker of the House of Commons is deeply embedded in English history and tradition, and is almost as old as Parliament itself. For over six hundred years the Speaker of the House has virtually ruled in the Chamber. The office originated in 1377, when Sir Thomas Hungerford was elected to speak on behalf of the Commons to King Edward III; and it has continued to the present day.

There are famous occasions when the Speaker has played a dramatic role in Parliament's history. On one occasion King Charles I came in person to the House to impeach five of his adversaries. Forewarned, they escaped as he approached Palace Yard. When he entered the House, he became the only monarch ever to cross the Bar. He said to the Speaker, Mr Lenthall, 'By your leave, Mr Speaker, I must borrow your chair a little.' When Charles realised he had arrived too late he said ruefully, 'Well since I see all the birds are flown, I do expect from you that you shall send them unto me as soon as they return.' He asked the Speaker if any of the five were still in the House, to which Lenthall replied: 'May it please Your Majesty, I have neither eyes to see nor tongue to speak in this place, but as the House is pleased to direct me, whose servant I am here; and I humbly beg Your Majesty's pardon, that I cannot give you any other answer than this to what Your Majesty is pleased to demand of me.' This was the first step towards the Independence of the House of Commons.

At the commencement of each Parliament, the Speaker still claims from the Queen the privilege of the Members of the House of Commons to have freedom of speech without threat of arrest. When a new Speaker is elected, he is ceremonially dragged to the Speaker's Chair by two senior back benchers. In centuries past the Speaker's office was at times dangerous and the Speaker in presenting unpleasant decisions to the King could risk losing his head. In those days, no one really wanted to be Speaker and the Member elected had to be dragged to the Chair. So today the custom persists, and the Speaker feigns reluctance to take office.

But today the Speaker of the House of Commons holds an extremely honoured position, sixth in precedence in England. The speaker is outranked only by the Royal Family, the Archbishop of Canterbury, the Archbishop of York, the Lord Chancellor, The Prime Minister and the Lord President of the Council.

The ten days following the notice of Selwyn Lloyd's retirement as Speaker were a period of intense activity, as each Party in the House decided whom they wanted as Speaker. For George Thomas, the Deputy Speaker, those ten days were almost ten years as he wondered what his future held. When the decision was taken, George was amazed and moved to discover that all eight parties had voted for him, and he was unanimously elected Speaker of the House.

In his memoirs, Harold Wilson describes how the

election came about:

'The Conservatives and Liberals let us know that they would support our choice of George Thomas, since March 1974 Chairman of Ways and Means and Deputy Speaker. His election was a matter of great delight to me. In the late forties I had seen him successfully presiding over the House, sitting on a Committee of Ways and Means on the annual finance Bill.... He was appointed as a member of the panel of Deputy Chairmen of Ways and Means, recruited for its successive stages, and this was where he first proved his ability in the Parliamentary chair. As a very young minister I decided that if I were ever in a position to influence the choice of Speaker in a later generation I should support him. Not many would have regarded him as Speaker material in those days. In his own Church and in Wales he was well known as a somewhat outlandish left-winger, often away from Westminster, once turning up somewhere on the wrong side of the Communist lines in Greece. But as a minister from October 1964 to June 1970 he had impressed the House as equally successful in the Home Office as an Under-Secretary of State, at the Commonwealth Office as Minister of State, and at the Welsh Office as Secretary of State. In that capacity he had to play a leading part at the Investiture of the Prince of Wales in Caernarvon Castle on 1 July 1969.'

In 1976 George Thomas became the one hundred and thirty third Speaker of the House, and only the second Labour MP elected to this honoured position. He says, 'I couldn't help thinking that I came to this House, a miner's son with my family living in Tonypandy. What a marvellous country this is that someone like me can come to this place without powerful friends and without wealth, and yet be given the trust of the whole House, for a Speaker can only function properly if he had the trust of the whole house.'

In some ways the office of Speaker can be very lonely, as the Speaker must be seen to be totally impartial. For this reason, the Speaker does not go into the Members' Smoke Room, bar or tearoom, and even stays out of the library. The tradition of the Commons is such that wherever the Speaker goes in the House, Members bow and step to one side to allow him to pass. It could have been very lonely for the new Speaker, for George Thomas loves company and has many friends on both sides of the House. His charm and friendliness have brought a new warmth to the office of Speaker.

The Speaker's procession, which takes place every day that Parliament is in session, is one of the great traditions of the House. Visitors and MPs may be mingling in the Central Lobby of the Houses of Parliament, but a few moments before 2.30 p.m. conversation is silenced. Echoing down the corridor leading to the Speaker's apartments comes the cry 'Speaker.' Everyone stands and the command is given, 'Hats off, strangers', Then in solemn dignity the Speaker and his retinue arrive in the Central Lobby. Only members of Parliament bow as the Speaker passes, everyone else, whatever their position in life, is a 'stranger' here. Leading this daily procession is the mace-bearer in his court dress, carrying the golden mace, the symbol of the Speaker's authority in the House, followed by the Speaker, and his officials and chaplain.

Passing through the Central Lobby, the Speaker turns right and moves on to enter the Chamber. Although George Thomas is not a lawyer, he wears the full-bottomed wig and robes of a Queen's Counsel, with black knee-breeches, black stockings and buckled shoes. During the six hundred years of the Speaker's office, there have only been seven who were not from the legal profession. By wearing these robes, it is made clear that the Speaker dispenses justice in the House of Commons.

Yet even amid the traditions and dignity of such an office, George Thomas is as unpretentious as ever. Spending most his time in the Chamber or in the Speaker's apartments, for he must be on call at all times from Monday to Friday, George Thomas still enjoys his weekends when he returns to his bungalow in Cardiff.

The Staterooms of Speaker's House are magnificent and it is here that distinguished foreign visitors and guests are entertained. As he looks at the opulence of this suite of rooms, he says, 'This is very different from what I was used to in Tonypandy.' The Speaker's Dining Room and Drawing Room are lined with portraits of past Speakers. Under each life-size portrait is the Speaker's personal coat of arms, and in the Drawing Room hangs George Thomas's portrait, underneath which is his own somewhat unusual coat of arms, reminding all who see it of his origins. The coat of arms incorporates the crown and portcullis design of the House of Commons, but is surmounted by a miner's lamp. The lower half of the coat of arms includes an open Bible. The motto is in Welsh. 'Bid ben bid bont' which means, 'He who would be a leader must be a bridge.'

Speaker's House used to be a residence on a grand scale, the ground floor consisting of large kitchens, store-rooms, and staff quarters. A fine staircase leads from Speaker's Court to the first floor where the State Rooms are situated. They consist of a large dining room where thirty-six people can be seated comfortably at the large table, a drawing room, and two smaller rooms with connecting doors. There used also to be an extensive library. Above were the main bedrooms, dressing rooms, and bathrooms. On the next floor were a mixture of odd-shaped rooms with connecting stairs. Today almost the entire cellar level and the Speaker's library have been given to the House of Commons Library. The State Rooms remain, but because the Speaker has to use one of the smaller drawing-rooms as his study, the drawing-room of the adjacent Serjeant at Arms' House has been added to the Speaker's quarters.

The Speaker's personal accommodation is now limited to the bedroom level. It is magnificently sited, overlooking the River Thames, the Lords' and the Commons' Terraces, and with views of Lambeth Palace, County Hall, the Festival Hall and other famous buildings.

George Thomas begins each day by reading a wide selection of newspapers. He has never forgotten that as a student he was called 'a very foolish young man' by his professor when he confessed to reading only one newspaper.

In the Chamber, the Speaker's first duty is to preserve order and dignity in the House's proceedings. He has extensive powers. He can call Members to order if they use unparliamentary language, for unbecoming behaviour, for irrelevance, and for unnecessary repetitiousness. He can tell Members to take their seats, or to take back words or a phrase. He can even order a Member from the Chamber. If he is not obeyed, he 'names' the offender, at which point a motion is put to suspend the member from service of the House. If he does not leave, he can be forcibly ejected by doorkeepers or messengers under the control of the Serjeant at Arms, at the Speaker's orders.

Should there be grave disorder in the House, the Speaker may adjourn or suspend the sitting. On four days in the week, the subject of the Adjournment Debate at the end of the day's business is selected by ballot. But on the fifth day, it falls to the Speaker to choose. He also selects topics for discussion on the motion for the adjournment, which takes most of the last day's sitting before a recess. The Speaker also chooses back-bench speakers from each side of the House. The duties of the Speaker are not only as the impartial Chairman of the House of Commons, but extend to all matters of accommodation and services needed for the smooth running of the House of Commons.

Prior to the sitting of Parliament, Mr Speaker faces much preparation. Members who wish to speak give prior notice of Private Notice questions; the Government indicates if there is to be a Ministerial statement. The Speaker must know the qualifications of those who wish to be called to speak, and while it is usual for the Speaker's Office to note the names of Members, it is the Speaker who has the final right to decide who speaks in the Chamber.

From time to time Mr Speaker receives complaints from Members usually by letter, asking why he has not been called to speak, or complaining that he has not been correctly reported in Hansard. The Speaker must then look into the matter, and intervene where necessary.

In preparing for the day's business, Mr Speaker has a briefing meeting at twelve noon every day that Parliament is sitting. At this meeting the business proposed for the day is discussed, and any procedure difficulties are ironed out. This is followed by a private meeting of the Speaker and his deputies, to plan for presiding in the Chamber.

However the Speaker's work is not concerned only with the Chamber. He is in effect at the helm of the administration of the House of Commons. He is the chairman of the House of Commons Commission, a body of Members which collectively employs all the staff of the House. It is to Mr Speaker and the Commission that the problems of any department are referred, whether dealing with library facilities or office accommodation.

Basically the administration has five departments, over all of which Mr Speaker has jurisdiction. There is the Clerks' Department, responsible for all matters relating to the Chamber. The second department is concerned with the 'house-keeping' and includes the provision of furniture, stationery and security; this is the Serjeant's Department. Responsible for the care and cataloguing of hundreds of thousands of books is the Library Depart-

ment, which has a research function for any Member of
the House, especially for Opposition MPs, for whom it acts
in the same way as civil servants do for the Government.
Charged with keeping records of everything said in
Parliament and in Standing Committees is the Official
Report Department, or Hansard as it is usually called. It is
named after T. C. Hansard, who undertook the work of
reporting debates in 1811, and whose family kept the work
going for almost eighty years. Finally there is the Administration Department itself, which looks after the needs of
all the other departments.

The Houses of Parliament are of course shared between
the House of Commons and the House of Lords. Thus the
use of Westminster Hall for any function is by joint consent
of the Speaker, on behalf of the Commons, and of the
Lord Chancellor and Lord Great Chamberlain for the
Lords.

Mr Speaker is the titular head of the Commons, and as
such deals with foreign governments in Parliamentary
relations, as distinct from diplomatic relations. The
Speaker's office takes great care in handling Parliamentary
relations with other governments, and this can sometimes
lead to differences of opinion with the Foreign Office. The
Speaker is also ex officio President of two organisations
involved in Parliamentary relations with foreign countries.
The Commonwealth Parliamentary Association, and the
Inter-Parliamentary Union. Every May, the Commonwealth Parliamentary Association holds a seminar lasting
between four and six weeks at which presiding officers
come to be instructed in the workings of the Mother of
Parliaments. It is the Speaker's duty to entertain these
guests and to speak to them.

Of course there are also return visits, when the British
Speaker visits overseas. Now that Britain is in the
European Community, the Speaker is invited to attend

conferences of the working parties of the European Parliament. He also attends official functions such as the opening of the new Parliamentary buildings in Strasbourg.

The Conference of Commonwealth Ministers takes place every two years, and the Speaker acts as chairman, or is represented on the committee organising each successive conference. The Speaker's work in the Chair in the House is really only the tip of the iceberg of his many official duties. Into this far-reaching and distinguished position George Thomas was thrust in 1976. It seemed a universe away from teaching in the dreary classroom of Roath Park School, yet he remains as unpretentions as ever.

As if these official duties were not enough, George Thomas still fulfils many engagements involving teachers' unions, Welsh affairs and church organisations. In the summer of 1979 he went to a Welsh singing festival, not in the valleys of Wales, but at Niagara, U.S.A.! He is still a preacher, much in demand for his sermons. His secretary, Sir Noel Short comments, 'He has a very busy life outside Parliament, and at times it is exhausting for a man of his age.' It is of course in the Chamber that George Thomas is seen publicly in action. 'Before I enter the Chamber, I always pray for wisdom, guidance and for God's help.' As Speaker he has an arduous task, and needs to know the names and to recognise each of the 635 MPs. This is quite a problem, as the House is often crowded, and Members address the House from where they stand. To preserve the concept of debate by conversation, the Chamber is small, permitting a sense of intimacy lost in larger auditoriums. The initial impact of the Chamber to a first-time visitor is its smallness. Although there are 635 Members, there is seating for only 400. When it's realised that thirty of forty Members may stand to try to catch the Speaker's eye, and thus be called to speak, the difficulty of calling a Member by name, and yet being fair to all points of view, can be imagined. yet without hesitation George Thomas, who has memorised every Member's name, calls on individuals to speak from the Government and Opposition benches alternately.

In many ways the Speaker is the focal point of the Commons. He sits in the centre of the Chamber towards one end, where his position commands a view of all the Members. The Speaker's Chair is large, and upholstered in green leather, as are the benches. It is backed by carved woodwork, and has a large canopy surmounted by the lion and unicorn crest.

The Speaker's Chair is raised above the table on which the despatch boxes rest, one on the Government side another on the Opposition side. The front benches are quite close together, only about twelve feet apart, but running between them for the length of the Chamber are two broad red strips in the carpet. These are the 'sword lines', and date from the earliest days of Parliament, when in the heat of debate, two opponents might draw their swords, but could not reach each other without crossing the line. Even today, if a Member while speaking steps over the line on his side of the Chamber, he is immediately called to order. In the cloakroom where it was expected that Members would leave their swords, each one had a silken loop provided on which to hang his sword; the loops are still there today. The rule is still no weapons in the House. An MP may not take a brief case into the Chamber; even if for reasons of health a Member wishes to take a walking-stick in, he may only do so by special consent.

George Thomas has impressed his own personality on proceedings in the House. At times his humour has defused an angry exchange of harsh words, and at other times, he has sternly reminded the House of its dignity and honour. One such event occurred after George Thomas had been the Speaker for only six weeks. It was a difficult situation which demanded swift action. The Labour Government had introduced the Aircraft and Shipbuilding Bill, which proposed nationalising these industries. As Speaker, George Thomas ruled that this was a Hybrid Bill in Parliamentary terms, since he did not feel that it dealt fairly with all aspects of the matter. This upset the sponsors of the Bill and the Government decided to press on with it. An Opposition amendment was tabled, when the results of the Divisions were announced there was confusion. It is customary for the tellers from the division lobbies to line up in front of the table to announce the result; it is always the teller from the winning party who stands on the right facing the Speaker. Therefore it is immediately obvious to Members even before any announcement who has won. On this occasion there was a tied vote, with Government and Opposition exactly equal. In such an event, the Speaker has the casting vote and the crowded Chamber waited to see what would happen. With no hesitation, George Thomas voted against the amendment, and it was lost. He did not vote against the Conservative amendment because of his own Party affiliations, for he is determined to be impartial as Speaker. He was following the precedent that, in the event of a tied vote the Speaker always votes against a one time Motion, that has no further stage to be considered, without regard to who proposed it. This stems from 1867, when the Speaker said that an important motion must have the majority of the House; if the House did not give such a majority, it was not for the presiding officer to make up the mind of the House. Therefore his vote must be with those against the motion. George Thomas quoted this, and in his vote followed its precedent.

The next step for the Speaker was to put to the House the main question, the Third Reading of the Bill. This was not just important for the aircraft and shipbuilding industries, for if the Government was defeated it could lead to a general election. It was expected that this too would be a tied vote and Mr Speaker would again follow precedent and vote against the motion, and the Labour government be defeated. This was not an easy decision for George Thomas, Labour Member for Cardiff West to make. But when the votes were taken and the tellers gave the results, the House was amazed. An extra vote for the Government had been found, and the Bill was carried by one vote, absolving George Thomas from following Speaker Denison's precedent in 1867.

Pandemonium broke out, as Members savoured victory or tasted defeat. The House had been crowded, and now more that 600 MPs tried to leave the Chamber. The door from the Chamber is quite narrow, and it was difficult to get out. George Thomas describes it as, 'like trying to get out of Cardiff Arms Park after a Rugby International.' Tempers were high, and one or two scuffles broke out, although George Thomas, in the Speaker's Chair, did not see them.

A few members decided to wait in the Chamber until the crowd had left, instead of struggling through the exit. As they waited, some excited Labour MPs, relieved at the result, began to sing, 'The Red Flag'. This so infuriated Michael Heseltine of the Conservative Front Bench that he ran and picked up the mace which stood on the table and waved it in the air. At this point George Thomas rose to his feet and suspended the sitting of the House for twenty minutes, the first Speaker to do so because of disrespect to the mace since the 1930's.

This occurred just after 10 o'clock in the evening, and the House was due to rise at 10.30 p.m. After suspending the sitting, George Thomas left and went to his apartments. Like a prairie fire, the news spread through the House. When he returned, the Chamber was packed to capacity. Members were standing beyond the bar of the House (a red

line across the carpet at the far end from Mr Speaker).
Another group was packed behind and around the
Speaker's Chair, and yet more were sitting in the aisles
between the tiers of crowded benches. The atmosphere was
subdued as Mr Speaker took his place. The Chamber
became silent, and the Member who had seized the mace
stood to apologise to the House. Before he could begin, Mr
Speaker stood and suspended the sitting again, until the
next day. It was a lesson that the dignity of the House must
be upheld.

The next day, Friday, the business of the House
commenced at 11 a.m., and although the Chamber is
usually fairly empty on Fridays, because MPs return to
their constituencies, on this morning a large crowd awaited
Mr Speaker. After prayers, which are said every day in the
Chamber, the first item of business was for the Member
who had taken the mace to apologise to the House. The
atmosphere was very different from the previous evening,
and people had had time to think the matter over. The
offending Member apologised sincerely and George
Thomas was going to let the matter rest.

At this point Eric Heffer, the Member for Walton,
Liverpool called: 'Point of Order, Mr Speaker.' Having
received consent to speak, he asked if the Speaker was
going to say or do anything further about the events of the
previous night. In reply, George Thomas said that the
House was the Mother of Parliaments, and what had
happened was a disgraceful lowering of standards. He
hoped he would never again see anything like it. The
House was very subdued as George Thomas made it clear
that it was now a closed matter.

On one occasion, some Labour back-benchers jeered a
Scots Nationalist women MP who rose to speak wearing a
bright pink, green, and blue dress.' The House should
welcome a little colour', said the Speaker gallantly.

As the months went by, George Thomas grew in the respect of Members of all Parties in the House. His mastery of procedure and his impartiality gained him great popularity. He could be firm, calling 'Order, Order' like the schoolmaster he used to be, and at other times by his humour saving the House from a bitter exchange of words.

George Thomas was in the Chair when Eddie Loyden, a Member from Liverpool was speaking. Business was proceeding amicably, when a Scottish Member, Mrs Ewing, now a Member of the European Parliament, called out on a point of order. When George Thomas asked her the reason, she said with her obvious Scottish accent, 'I cannot understand a single word that the honourable gentleman is saying!' Eddie Loyden who obviously had a Merseyside accent was incensed, as were his friends in the Tribune group. Comments and suggestions flew back and forth across the Chamber. 'Order, Order', called George Thomas, with his Welsh intonation. But the shouting continued. Then he stood up. When the Speaker stands, everyone must sit and be silent. George Thomas looked around the Chamber severely, and then said with perhaps a little more Welsh inflection than usual, 'There are many accents in this House. I only wish I had one myself.' There was a moment's silence, then Eddie Loyden dissolved in laughter, and the whole House roared in amusement. George Thomas sat back, the good humour of the House had been restored.

Of course there are times when a Member uses unparliamentary language, and the Speaker asks that the phrase be withdrawn. It always is. For example, no one may call another Member, 'a liar'. Sometimes such words may be used in the heat of the moment, but are withdrawn immediately – sometimes alternative phrases are substituted. Winston Churchill was once rebuked for referring to a Member telling lies, and the Speaker interrupted. Mr

Churchill said, 'Yes I withdraw the phrase', but went on, 'The honourable gentleman was guilty of a terminological inexactitude.'

For visitors to the House, Question Time is possibly the most interesting, and especially Questions to the Prime Minister. Members seek to score Party points, particularly now it is broadcast on the radio. During this time the Speaker's expertise is often put to the test. One Question Time a very hesitant Member was taking a long time. 'Come on, come on' shouted other Members, only adding to the questioner's confusion. 'Order,' called George Thomas, and looking at the hesitant member said, 'You are taking longer to ask the question than I used to take.' Older members laughed, remembering that as a young Welsh MP, George Thomas's questions were very long indeed.

He has a simple philosophy about humour, and never uses his position to his advantage. When George Thomas jokes, it is always on himself. 'If a Member is slighted, the one making the joke soon forgets, and the House soon forgets, but the one slighted never forgets. When I make a joke it is always on myself.'

George Thomas has also a wit which can achieve in a few words the result he wants. One Question Time, a Member wanted to follow his question with suggestions as to a future course of action, and embarking on a speech began, 'I suggest that . . .' At this point Mr Speaker interrupted: 'This is Question Time not Suggestion Time', effectively cutting the Member short.

During questions to the Prime Minister it is permitted to ask questions only on matters for which the Prime Minister has responsibility. Recently a Member wanted to ask Mrs Thatcher about the activities of certain Labour Members. George Thomas disallowed the question on the grounds that she could not answer for Members of another party. 'But Mr Speaker', persisted the questioner, 'It's in today's newspapers.' George Thomas retorted, 'So is my horoscope.'

It is easy for Members who feel strongly on a subject to get carried away and speak for a long time. The Speaker whilst having almost absolute power with the Chamber, has no right to stop a Member speaking, no matter how long he has been doing so. On one well-reported occasion, Harold Lever was called to speak about 11.30 a.m. on a Friday morning, and was still going strong at 4 p.m. in the afternoon. He was seeking to talk out a proposal.

If a Member is going on too long, the Speaker waits for an interruption; 'and someone will always interrupt', he comments with a smile. The usual form of interruption is 'Will the honourable gentleman give way?' George Thomas will stand which focuses on his Chair, and say, 'it is very unfair to interrupt the honourable gentleman, who has already been speaking twenty three minutes.' A slight emphasis on 'twenty three' is enough to make the Member realise he has been going on too long!

It is the courtesies which are the strength of the House, and if a Member participates in a debate, he is expected to sit through it. Of course there are occasions when urgent business means he must leave the Chamber, but he is expected to be present for the end of the debate.

As Speaker, George Thomas tries to be fair about calling Members to speak. 'If one Member has spoken nine times in the session and another only once, it's obvious where the precedence must lie. Everybody is entitled to have their constituents know they are playing their part here.

It is the Speaker's task to rule whether a motion about alleged breach of privilege or contempt of the House should receive priority over other parliamentary business. The modern usage is for the Speaker to take twenty-four hours to give consideration to the question. If he decides in favour of priority, a motion is normally put that the matter be referred to the Committee of Privileges, a Select Committee of the House. On a few occasions, the matter is dealt with there and then by the House of Commons.

George Thomas' duties as Speaker are very wide and he is always busy. Members of all Parties seek his advice; whatever is said privately to the Speaker is kept in the strictest confidence. He is often consulted on matters of procedure by Commonwealth Governments.

As Speaker, he does not remain in the Chair for every hour of debate, but after two or three hours in the Chamber, delegates the chairmanship to one of three Deputy Speakers, returning during the evening for the final speeches. When there is a major question in the House, or great tension over a Bill, George Thomas will remain in control, exercising authority in his inimitable way. When the debate over the Devolution of Scotland Bill was in progress, George Thomas remained in the Speaker's Chair for nine hours.

George Thomas served with great distinction as Speaker until 1979 when a General Election was called. Even as Speaker of the House he still holds his regular 'surgeries' in Cardiff West, when those with grievances can see him, and he does all in his power to help. In the Commons, Members bow in deference, but in Cardiff he is still 'Our George.'

It is the custom that at a General Election the Speaker of the House is returned unopposed. But at the 1979 Election two parties defied this tradition and put forward candidates to oppose him. When the count was announced, the candidates of the Welsh Nationalist and the National Front had been overwhelmingly defeated, and George Thomas went back to Westminister with a huge majority, giving him the largest percentage increase of any MP, this against the background of a Conservative victory.

He wondered what about his position, since there was now a Conservative government under the leadership of Margaret Thatcher. But for him, there was no change. George Thomas had gained the respect, affection and trust of Parliament by his fair-minded chairmanship, his friendly and courteous manner, and his masterly handling of debates.

In the new Parliament, all the political parties wanted him to continue as Speaker. Mrs Thatcher in her first speech in the new Parliament as Prime Minister said, 'Mr Speaker, we always thought that you would be one of our great Speakers, and you are.' One of his first tasks was to memorize from photographs, the faces of 130 new Members. He was determined to know each one, never having forgotten that as a young MP about to make his maiden speech, he was called, 'Mr Roberts.' George Thomas was not going to embarrass any new MP.

The Right Honourable George Thomas returned to his familar place in the Speaker's Chair to which Mrs Thatcher welcomed him. 'We shall continue to be in need of your kindness, wisdom and integrity.' The man from the Rhondda valley acknowledged the compliment and in his unmistakeable Welsh accent called, 'Order! Order!' Parliament continued its business.

Appendix

The present Speaker, Rt Hon George Thomas MP in presiding over the House of Commons is constantly aware of, and takes great pride in the long traditions of the House.

Parliament emerged during the late 13th and early 14th centuries because of the growing need for a superior court to deal with legal and administrative situations at a national level.

The early Parliaments had as their basis the officers of the King's household, the King's judges and ecclesiastical dignitaries and officers whom the King might summon from time to time, and occasionally knights of the realm. The Commons were summoned to all the Parliaments of Edward III and by the conclusion of his reign a House of Commons was beginning to emerge. In 1377 the first known Speaker was elected.

There have been many changes in the intervening centuries, one of the most far reaching was the development of the idea that the Speaker would be totally impartial. The Speaker of the House was formerly partisan in his views but between 1728 (Speaker Onslow) and 1839

(Speaker Shaw Lefevre) the fact of the Speaker's impartiality was developed. Now Mr Speaker neither speaks in debates nor votes except in the event of an equal vote in the House.

Changes have occurred in the House itself too. The original palace of Westminster was built by Edward the Confessor but was burned down in 1834, except for Westminster Hall. It was replaced by the present building in 1850 built by Sir Charles Barry.

The Chamber of the House of Commons in this building was totally destroyed on May 10th 1941 in a German bombing raid. Winston Churchill is said to have wept when he saw the damage next morning, but said pugnaciously, 'Parliament shall not lose a day's debate!' The Commons moved overnight to Church House, Westminster, which is situated at the rear of the Abbey.

The Chamber of the House of Commons was rebuilt and completed in 1950, but as a perpetual reminder of the dark days of 1941, the arch at the entrance to the Chamber, smoke blackened and scarred by bomb splinters was taken down stone by stone and stored until the war was over. It was then rebuilt into the new Chamber. The marks of war-time devastation still on its stones contrast sharply with the newer building. By unanimous approval it is called 'The Churchill Arch.'

The new Chamber is substantially furnished by gifts of all kinds sent by the commonwealth countries and colonies of that time.

Recent Lakeland paperbacks

GOD'S LAST WORD
Jim Packer

Is the Bible all true? And is it important that it should be? Jim Packer, the bestselling author of KNOWING GOD, takes a decisive stand on these questions. But he goes beyond the issue of inerrancy to the more important one of authority – what is the point of winning the battle for the Bible if in the process we lose our understanding of its role? The Bible is central to both personal and public worship. To recover truly biblical faith and practice we need to restore the Bible to its rightful place in the lives of present-day Christians and churches.

Writing with a deep pastoral concern Jim Packer brings us back to devotion and worship as the key to understanding God's word and appropriating it for ourselves. GOD'S LAST WORD is a challenging reminder that it is nothing less than our souls which are at stake in this debate.

WHY I BELIEVE
D. James Kennedy

Do you know what Christians believe, and why they believe it? Can you defend your belief against the critics all around you?

Dr D. James Kennedy, the world renowned founder of Evangelism Explosion International, was so angry when he heard a militant atheist make mincemeat out of the Christian callers-in to a radio talk show he had to do something. From his lifetime of study he has brought together a compellingly powerful declaration of what Christians believe and why...intelligent, informed responses to frequently heard objections to the Christian faith.

Intensely penetrating and personal, this book is a statement you will want to make your own.

Recent Lakeland paperbacks

SOMETIMES MOUNTAINS MOVE
C. Everett & Elizabeth Koop

This is a journal of one Christian family's ordeal with death – the loss of their twenty-year-old son while mountain climbing. 'Is the grace of God sufficient at a time like this and under these circumstances?' write C. Everett and Elizabeth Koop. 'Your gentle son, presumed dead, tied to the sheer face of a cliff hundreds of feet above the valley floor, the temperature below freezing, and the only person who could possibly shed any light on the matter lying under sedation in hospital. Yes, the grace of God was sufficient . . .'

Here is a sensitive chronicle of faith amid despair, in the tradition of C. S. Lewis's 'A Grief Observed'.

HOW SHOULD WE THEN LIVE?
Francis A. Schaeffer

As one of the foremost evangelical thinkers of our day, Dr Schaeffer has long pondered the fate of declining Western culture, and concludes that not only have we lost sight of our roots, but of our direction as well. However, unlike most doomsayers, he pinpoints the problems, researches their origins and formulates a hopeful, positive proposal for the future.

Dr Schaeffer begins his brilliant analysis with the fall of Rome, tracing Western man's progression throughout the ensuing ages. From ancient Roman times to the Middle Ages, through the Renaissance, the Reformation and the Enlightenment, up to our present scientific Atomic Age, each step of our cultural development is scrutinized, documented and expanded upon in the light of subsequent historical facts. This is a penetrating and personal book from which readers can draw intellectual strength and moral encouragement.

Recent Lakeland paperbacks

THE GOLDEN COW
Materialism in the Twentieth-century Church
John White

Is it possible that the church today has begun worshipping the golden cow of materialism and success? John White begins to answer this question by considering the property-centred outlook of many churches whose evangelistic and church-building endeavours are governed more by mass psychology than by prayerful planning. Then he examines the fund-raising techniques of Christian organizations. Turning to Christian businesses, he asks whether they have become desensitized to what is sacred. Finally, the author moves into the frequently statistic-ridden realm of evangelism. In this prophetic book John White asks us to consider whether we, too, are worshipping the golden cow.

"I believe this book is destined to be one of the most upsetting, thoughtprovoking, and powerful books of this decade." – *George Verwer*

SOLD OUT
Clive Calver

Clive Calver, National Director of British Youth for Christ, takes the lid off evangelism. He argues that the church has learned to imitate the advertising techniques of modern-day society, and so often the evangelist descends to the level of being no more than a door-to-door salesman of ready-packaged, bargain-offer religion. By slick selling techniques he seeks to convert the world, but far from turning the world upside down the opposite has occurred.

This book explains how we can return to the dynamic witness of the early church and see our churches grow, emphasising that Jesus' call was 'Go and make disciples' and not 'Go and make converts'.